DAYSKIPPI

Shore-Based Course N

WHAT THE WORDS MEAN ...

Sailing and boating, like all pastimes, has its own jargon. The beginner can get away with *'front and back'* for a while but will have to learn the 'right' words sooner or later.

The best place to learn is at sea, on a boat, but failing that, the first part of this booklet should give you an idea of how to interpret the language sailors love to use.

The rest of the booklet is aimed at illustrating and clarifying the shore-based courses run by the Royal Yachting Association.

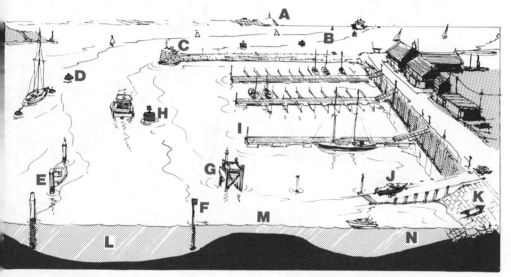

A **HEADLAND** prominent land sticking out into the seas.

B **FAIRWAY** main channel into harbour

C **BREAKWATER** sea wall

D **MOORING BUOYS** when laid in a line called TROTS.

E **PILE MOORINGS** posts driven into the seabed.

F **BEACON** Navigation mark not always lit.

G **DOLPHIN** structures used as navigation mark.

H **NAVIGATION BUOY** marks edge of channel (see page 54).

I **PONTOON** Floating platform to moor to — several together known as a *MARINA*.

J **SLIPWAY** Ramp to launch boats.

K **HARD** Solid ground to launch from.

L **CHANNEL** deep route.

M **SHOAL OR SHALLOWS**

N **SHELVING** How the sea bottom slopes — steep or gentle.

1. **DAVITS** — *(Crane for hoisting dinghy onboard)*

2. **COCKPIT**

3. **WHEEL HOUSE**

4. **INSIDE HELMSMANS POSITION**

5. **COCKPIT LOCKER** *(Cupboard)*

6. **COCKPIT SOLE** *(Floor)*

7. **FLYING BRIDGE OR FLYBRIDGE**

8. **RADAR ANTENNA**

9. **RADIO AERIAL**

10. **STANCHION**

11. **GUARD RAIL**

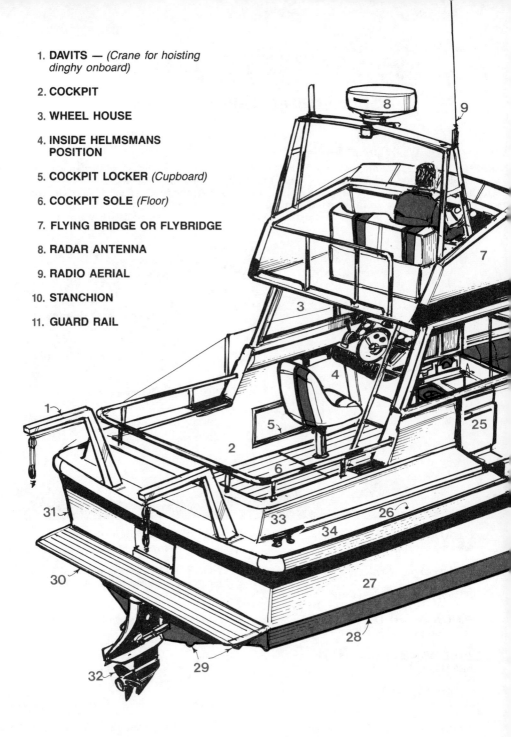

12. PULPIT

13. FENDERS

14. FAIRLEAD
(to pass ropes through)

15. BOW ROLLER *(for anchor line)*

16. WINDLASS *(Anchor winch)*

17. FORE DECK

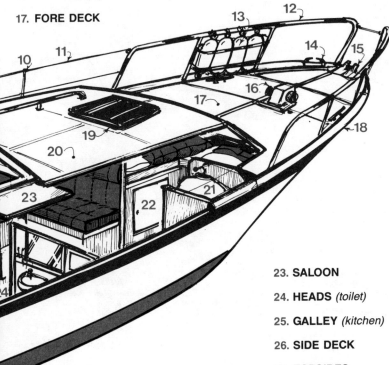

23. SALOON

24. HEADS *(toilet)*

25. GALLEY *(kitchen)*

26. SIDE DECK

27. TOPSIDES

28. CHINE
(corner between topsides & bottom)

29. RAIL OR SPRAYRAIL

30. BATHING PLATFORM

31. TRANSOM *(Flat back of boat)*

32. STERN OR OUTDRIVE

33. CLEAT

34. GUNWALE *(Top edge of hull)*

**18. RUBBING STRAKE
OR FENDERING**

19. HATCH

**20. COACH ROOF
or super structure**

21. HANGING LOCKER *(wardrobe)*

**22. FORECABIN
FOC'SLE**

SIMPLE HULL SHAPES

DISPLACEMENT
Whole hull pushes
through the water

SEMI-DISPLACEMENT
Part of the hull lifts
out at speed

PLANING
At high speed hull is riding
on the surface.

ROUND BILGE
Usual for displacement craft
that have to push through
the water.

HARD CHINE OR SHALLOW VEE
This shape will plane at high
speed but 'slams' in waves.

DEEP VEE
The *'Veed'* hull was
developed to maintain high
speeds in waves.

POWER

INBOARD ENGINE —
Drives a propeller on a shaft
— steers with a rudder.

OUTBOARD ENGINE
Drives its owns propeller and
steers by turning.

OUTDRIVE OR STERNDRIVE
Inboard engine powers a
steerable propeller or unit

TYPES

WEEKENDER

SPORTS DAY CRUISER

SPORTS FISHERMAN

FAST CRUISER

LONG-DISTANCE CRUISER

TRAWLER YACHT

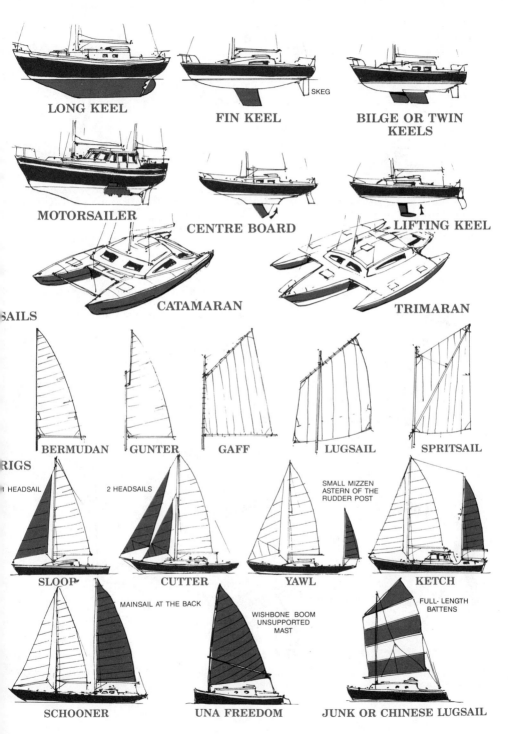

LONG KEEL

FIN KEEL SKEG

BILGE OR TWIN KEELS

MOTORSAILER

CENTRE BOARD

LIFTING KEEL

CATAMARAN

TRIMARAN

SAILS

BERMUDAN **GUNTER** **GAFF** **LUGSAIL** **SPRITSAIL**

RIGS

1 HEADSAIL   2 HEADSAILS

SMALL MIZZEN ASTERN OF THE RUDDER POST

SLOOP **CUTTER** **YAWL** **KETCH**

MAINSAIL AT THE BACK

WISHBONE BOOM UNSUPPORTED MAST

FULL-LENGTH BATTENS

SCHOONER **UNA FREEDOM** **JUNK OR CHINESE LUGSAIL**

VERY SIMPLE SAILING THEORY

A curved surface in an airflow creates *LOW PRESSURE* on one side and *HIGH PRESSURE* on the other.

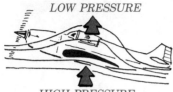

LOW PRESSURE

HIGH PRESSURE

An aircraft wing is 'SUCKED' and 'PUSHED' up as it makes an angle to the airflow

A sail is also 'SUCKED' and 'PUSHED' in a similar way to an aircraft wing

See for yourself how a spoon is 'SUCKED' by a fast water flow

WHY DOESN'T A BOAT GO SIDEWAYS?

As the wind is 'sucking' and 'pushing' on the sail trying to drive the boat sideways, as well as forwards, the water is 'pushing' back against the side of the boat.

The result of these forces is sometimes likened to a bar of soap shooting out when squeezed between two hands.

WHY DOESN'T THE BOAT BLOW OVER?

The wind spills out of the sail as it tips over and its force is counterbalanced by:-

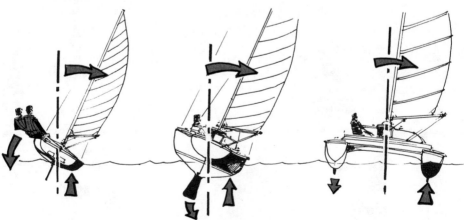

The weight of the crew plus the buoyancy of the immersed hull.

The weight of the keel plus the buoyancy of the immersed hull.

The weight of the boat plus the buoyancy of the other hull.

NAUTICAL TERMS

'PORT' and 'STARBOARD' are often confused — this little saying might help.

"The captain *LEFT* his *RED PORT* wine behind"

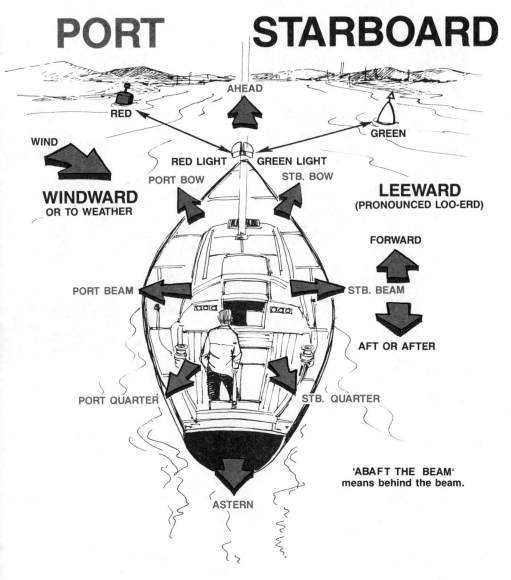

PORT

STARBOARD

AHEAD

RED

GREEN

WIND

WINDWARD
OR TO WEATHER

RED LIGHT   GREEN LIGHT

PORT BOW

STB. BOW

LEEWARD
(PRONOUNCED LOO-ERD)

FORWARD

PORT BEAM

STB. BEAM

AFT OR AFTER

PORT QUARTER

STB. QUARTER

'ABAFT THE BEAM'
means behind the beam.

ASTERN

7

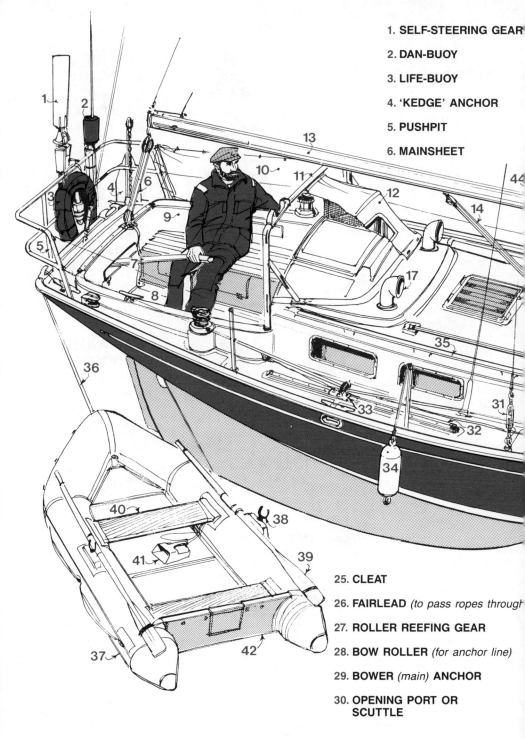

1. **SELF-STEERING GEAR**

2. **DAN-BUOY**

3. **LIFE-BUOY**

4. **'KEDGE' ANCHOR**

5. **PUSHPIT**

6. **MAINSHEET**

25. **CLEAT**

26. **FAIRLEAD** *(to pass ropes through*

27. **ROLLER REEFING GEAR**

28. **BOW ROLLER** *(for anchor line)*

29. **BOWER** *(main)* **ANCHOR**

30. **OPENING PORT OR SCUTTLE**

7. TILLER

8. COCKPIT

9. COCKPIT COAMING

10. DODGERS

11. BOOM GALLOWS

12. SPRAY HOOD

13. BOOM

14. KICKING STRAP

15. MAST

16. MAST PULPIT

17. VENTILATOR

18. STANCHIONS

19. FOREHATCH

20. COACH ROOF

21. FORE DECK

22. TOE-RAIL

23. PULPIT

24. WINDLASS *(winch)*

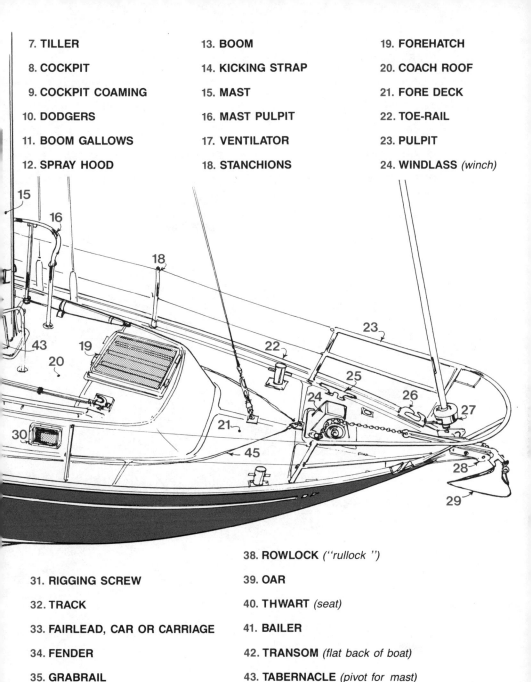

38. ROWLOCK *("rullock")*

31. RIGGING SCREW

32. TRACK

33. FAIRLEAD, CAR OR CARRIAGE

34. FENDER

35. GRABRAIL

36. PAINTER

37. TENDER *(dinghy)*

39. OAR

40. THWART *(seat)*

41. BAILER

42. TRANSOM *(flat back of boat)*

43. TABERNACLE *(pivot for mast)*

44. GOOSE-NECK *(Joint between mast & boom)*

45. JACK STAY *(to clip safety harness to)*

1. **AFTER DECK**

2. **LIFE-RAFT STOWAGE**

3. **GAS-LOCKER** *(cupboard)*

4. **COCKPIT LOCKER**

5. **COCKPIT SOLE** *(floor)*

6. **COMPANION WAY**
   (entrance to cabin)

7. **WASH BOARD** *(drop-in-boards)*

8. **MAIN HATCH**

9. **GUNWALE** *("gunnel") (top edge of boats side)*

10. **BOW** *(front of the boat)*

11. **STEM** *(sharp bit between deck & water)*

12. **FOREFOOT** *(where the stem & keel meet)*

13. **TOPSIDES** *(between water & deck)*

14. **BOOT TOP** *(painted band just above water)*

15. **WATERLINE**

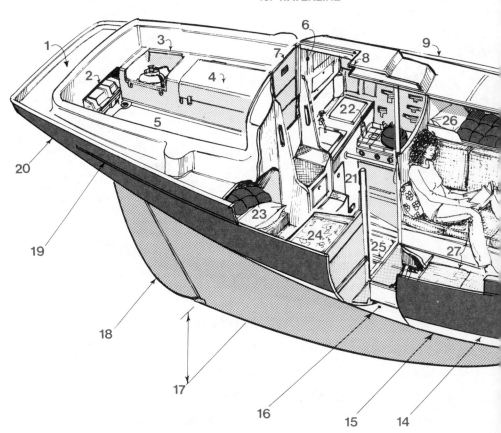

10

16. **BILGE** *(where the bottom joins the sides or space under the sole)*

17. **DRAFT** *(depth of water "what she draws")*

18. **RUDDER**

19. **CAVITA LINE** *(decorative line)*

20. **STERN** *(back end)*

21. **GALLEY** *(kitchen)*

22. **GIMBAL** *(pivot to keep stove level)*

23. **QUARTER BERTH** *(bed)*

24. **CHART TABLE**

25. **CABIN SOLE** *(floor)*

26. **PILOT BERTH** *(bed)*

27. **BUNK OR SETTEE BERTH**

28. **DECK HEAD** *(ceiling)*

29. **HANGING LOCKER**

30. **BULKHEAD** *(wall)*

31. **'HEADS'** *(toilet)*

32. **SEACOCK** *(valve to let water in or out)*

33. **FORECABIN, FOREPEAK, FOC'SLE**

34. **LEECLOTH** *(stops you falling out)*

35. **ANCHOR WELL**

36. **CHAIN PIPE**

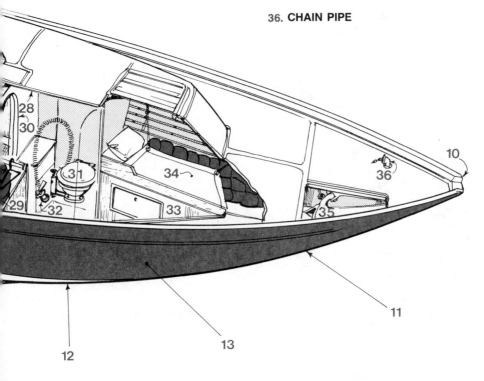

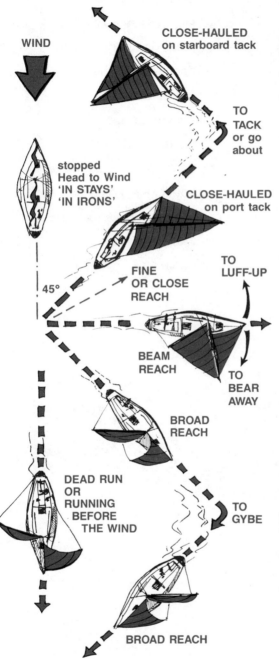

WIND

CLOSE-HAULED
on starboard tack

stopped
Head to Wind
'IN STAYS'
'IN IRONS'

CLOSE-HAULED
on port tack

TO
TACK
or go
about

45°

FINE
OR CLOSE
REACH

TO
LUFF-UP

BEAM
REACH

TO
BEAR
AWAY

BROAD
REACH

DEAD RUN
OR
RUNNING
BEFORE
THE WIND

TO
GYBE

BROAD REACH

POINTS OF SAIL AND SAILING TERMS

CLOSE HAULED is as close to the wind as the boat will sail (say about 45°)

To sail towards the wind a boat must **TACK** or zig-zag. (Also known as beating)

STARBOARD TACK is when the wind comes over the starboard side.

PORT TACK is when the wind comes over the port side.

TO TACK OR GO ABOUT is to change from one tack to the other by putting the bow through the wind.

FINE OR CLOSE REACH is a course between close-hauled and a beam reach.

TO LUFF-UP is to steer the boat towards the wind.

TO BEAR AWAY is to steer away from the wind.

BEAM REACH is when the wind comes over the beam (ie. 90°).

TO GYBE is to let the mainsail change sides by putting the sterm through the wind.

BROAD REACH is when the wind comes over the quarter.

DEAD RUN OR RUNNING BEFORE THE WIND is when the wind is blowing over the stern.

SAILS

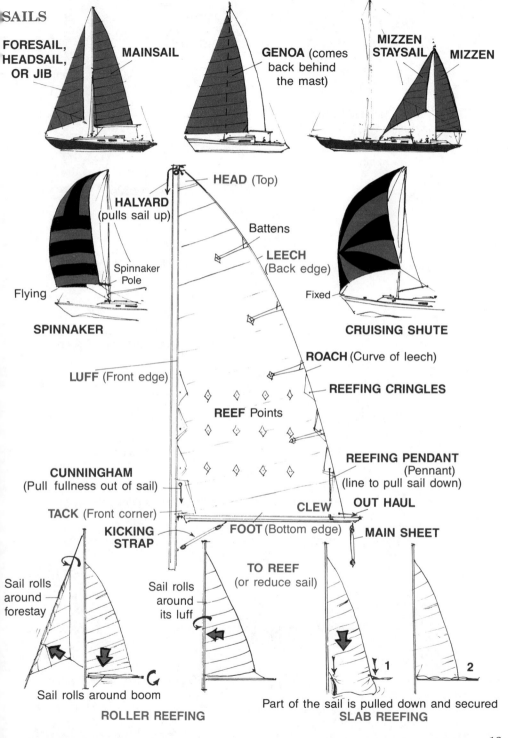

FORESAIL, HEADSAIL, OR JIB

MAINSAIL

GENOA (comes back behind the mast)

MIZZEN STAYSAIL

MIZZEN

HALYARD (pulls sail up)

HEAD (Top)

Battens

LEECH (Back edge)

Spinnaker Pole

Flying

SPINNAKER

Fixed

CRUISING SHUTE

ROACH (Curve of leech)

LUFF (Front edge)

REEFING CRINGLES

REEF Points

REEFING PENDANT (Pennant) (line to pull sail down)

CUNNINGHAM (Pull fullness out of sail)

TACK (Front corner)

CLEW

OUT HAUL

KICKING STRAP

FOOT (Bottom edge)

MAIN SHEET

Sail rolls around forestay

Sail rolls around its luff

TO REEF (or reduce sail)

Sail rolls around boom

ROLLER REEFING

1

2

Part of the sail is pulled down and secured
SLAB REEFING

RIGGING

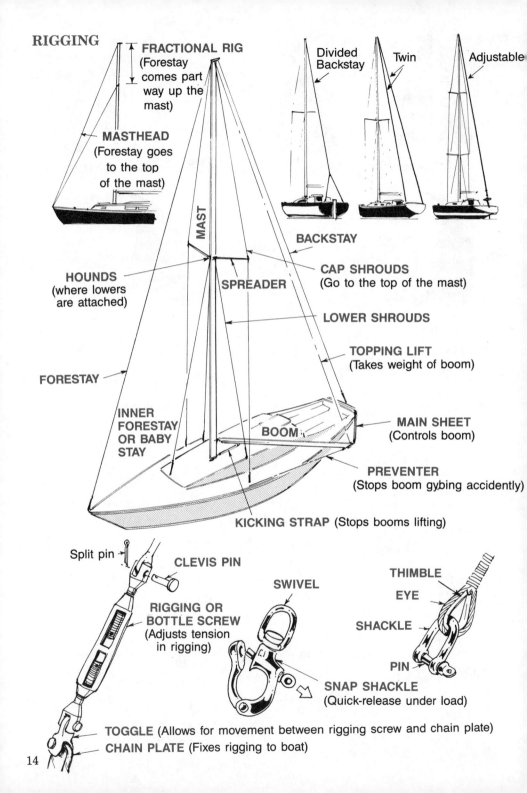

FRACTIONAL RIG (Forestay comes part way up the mast)

MASTHEAD (Forestay goes to the top of the mast)

Divided Backstay

Twin

Adjustable

MAST

BACKSTAY

HOUNDS (where lowers are attached)

SPREADER

CAP SHROUDS (Go to the top of the mast)

LOWER SHROUDS

TOPPING LIFT (Takes weight of boom)

FORESTAY

INNER FORESTAY OR BABY STAY

BOOM

MAIN SHEET (Controls boom)

PREVENTER (Stops boom gybing accidently)

KICKING STRAP (Stops booms lifting)

Split pin

CLEVIS PIN

SWIVEL

THIMBLE

EYE

RIGGING OR BOTTLE SCREW (Adjusts tension in rigging)

SHACKLE

PIN

SNAP SHACKLE (Quick-release under load)

TOGGLE (Allows for movement between rigging screw and chain plate)

CHAIN PLATE (Fixes rigging to boat)

ROPES *Modern ropes fall into four main types:-*

NYLON is very elastic which makes it ideal for anchor lines (absorbs shock).

POLYESTER (ICI Trade name Terylene) hardly stretches at all which makes it an ideal all round rope especially good for halyards.

POLYPROPYLENE (trade name Courlene) is a cheaper rope which also floats, good for dinghy painters and rescue lines.

KEVLAR is very strong and non-elastic, but expensive.

CONSTRUCTION

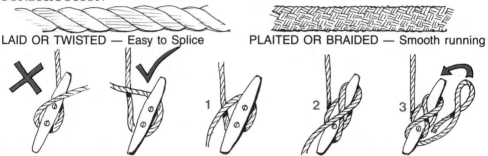

LAID OR TWISTED — Easy to Splice   PLAITED OR BRAIDED — Smooth running

TO MAKE FAST TO A CLEAT
1. Take a turn around the cleat. 2. Make several 'figure of 8' turns to build in some friction 3. Finish off *if necessary* with a 'twisted' loop to lock it.

STOWING A COIL

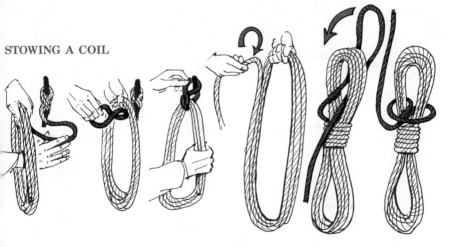

A halyard can be stowed
on the cleat like this.

Laid rope needs to be coiled
clockwise and given a *right hand*
twist in each turn. Then stowed
like this.

KNOTS

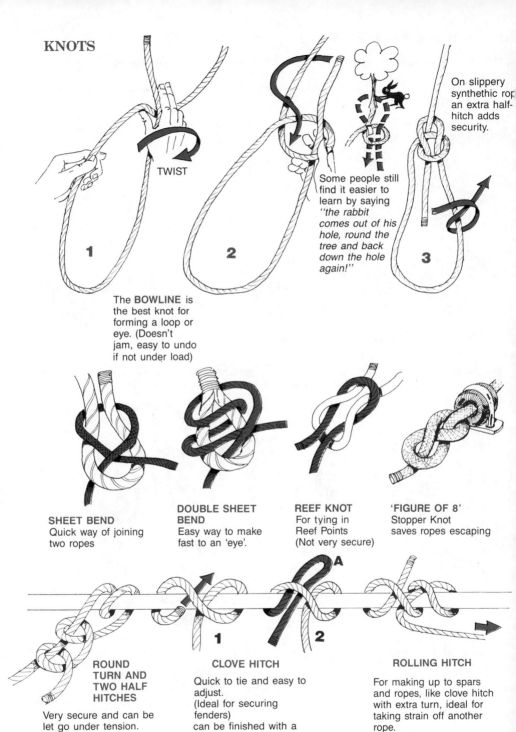

TWIST

1

2

On slippery synthethic rope an extra half-hitch adds security.

Some people still find it easier to learn by saying *"the rabbit comes out of his hole, round the tree and back down the hole again!"*

3

The **BOWLINE** is the best knot for forming a loop or eye. (Doesn't jam, easy to undo if not under load)

SHEET BEND
Quick way of joining two ropes

DOUBLE SHEET BEND
Easy way to make fast to an 'eye'.

REEF KNOT
For tying in Reef Points (Not very secure)

'FIGURE OF 8'
Stopper Knot saves ropes escaping

ROUND TURN AND TWO HALF HITCHES
Very secure and can be let go under tension. (Mooring lines)

CLOVE HITCH
Quick to tie and easy to adjust.
(Ideal for securing fenders)
can be finished with a loop (**A**) for quick-release

1

2

A

ROLLING HITCH
For making up to spars and ropes, like clove hitch with extra turn, ideal for taking strain off another rope.

16

ANCHORING

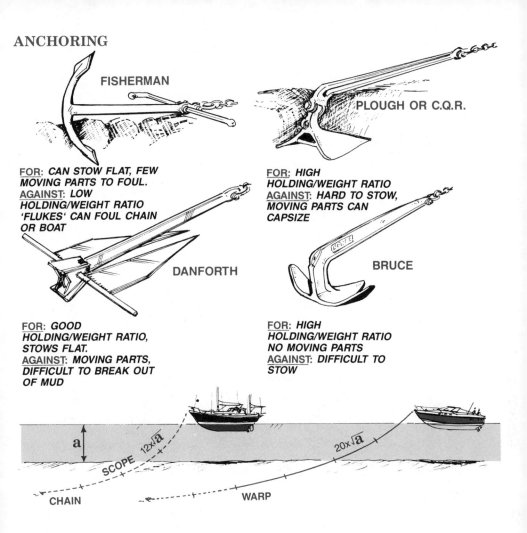

FISHERMAN

PLOUGH OR C.Q.R.

FOR: *CAN STOW FLAT, FEW MOVING PARTS TO FOUL.*
AGAINST: *LOW HOLDING/WEIGHT RATIO 'FLUKES' CAN FOUL CHAIN OR BOAT*

FOR: *HIGH HOLDING/WEIGHT RATIO*
AGAINST: *HARD TO STOW, MOVING PARTS CAN CAPSIZE*

DANFORTH

BRUCE

FOR: *GOOD HOLDING/WEIGHT RATIO, STOWS FLAT.*
AGAINST: *MOVING PARTS, DIFFICULT TO BREAK OUT OF MUD*

FOR: *HIGH HOLDING/WEIGHT RATIO NO MOVING PARTS*
AGAINST: *DIFFICULT TO STOW*

a

SCOPE 12x√a   20x√a

CHAIN   WARP

Whichever type of anchor you choose it will work best if the pull on it is close to horizontal. To achieve this the anchor line must be given plenty of 'SCOPE'.

If using chain the scope would be $12 \times \sqrt{max.\ depth\ of\ water\ expected\ in\ metres}$.

Nylon rope also absorbs shock but needs at least $20 \times \sqrt{the\ depth\ of\ water\ in\ metres}$ to give a fair pull on the anchor. A length of chain (at least 5m) near the anchor guards against chafe and helps the anchor dig in.

In bad weather where the boat is pitching and snatching a scope of 10 times the depth of water may be needed. *"If in doubt, let more out!"* chain does more good on the sea bottom than in your chain locker!

Simple 'rule of thumb' approximations for scope are, for chain, 4 x depth for warp, 6 x depth.

17

TRIPPING LINES

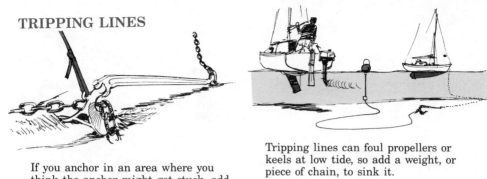

If you anchor in an area where you think the anchor might get stuck, add a tripping line to the other end. This lets you pull it clear if it jams.

Tripping lines can foul propellers or keels at low tide, so add a weight, or piece of chain, to sink it.

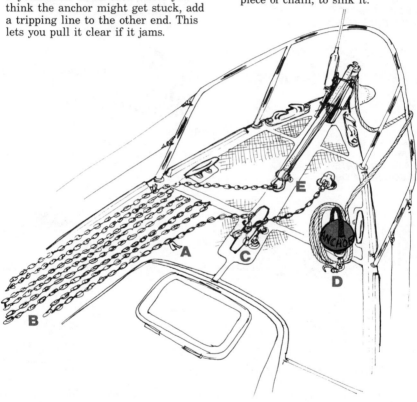

PREPARING TO ANCHOR
Good preparation can make all the difference:-

(A) Mark the chain to see how much to let out.
(B) Flaking the chain down prevents snarl-ups when you let go.
(C) Secure to the cleat so you can always let out more line.
(D) Rig a tripping line if you are worried about the anchor fouling on the bottom.
(E) *"Mouse"* shackle pin with wire to prevent it undoing as anchor moves on sea bed.

18

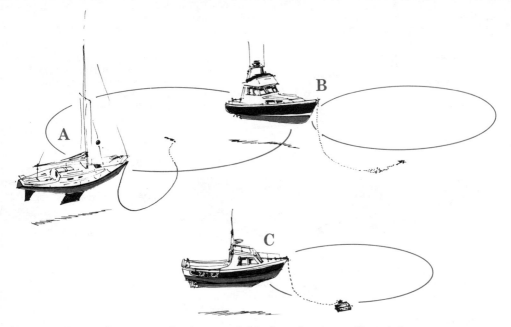

Choosing where to drop your anchor in a crowded harbour is not easy. Try to judge your neighbours swinging circles

(A) is a lightweight anchored with rope, so might 'sail' about in a large circle.

(B) is anchored with chain, but if not properly laid might just be lying to a 'heap' which will undo and increase his circle if the wind picks up. He also has a lot of windage on the hull and not much grip in the water, so could also 'sail' about in a blow.

(C) is a bit more predictable, heavy boat *moored* with chain.

MOORINGS AND ANCHORING MIXTURE

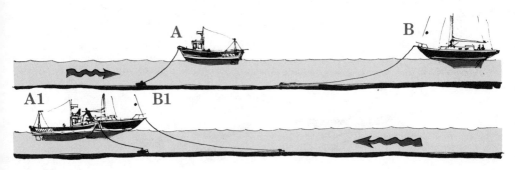

The scope of a permanent mooring (A) is less than that of a boat at anchor (B) so they won't swing the same amount when the tide turns (A1, B1).

USING FRICTION

The more turns you make with a rope the more friction you get. So very large forces can be controlled with the minimum of effort.
Winches use this principle.

USING WINCHES

Use only one turn to pull in the slack of jib sheet. Use more and it can jam.

As the load comes on the sheet add more turns to increase friction.

Use handle to increase leverage. Wind in sheet and secure to cleat.

RELEASING

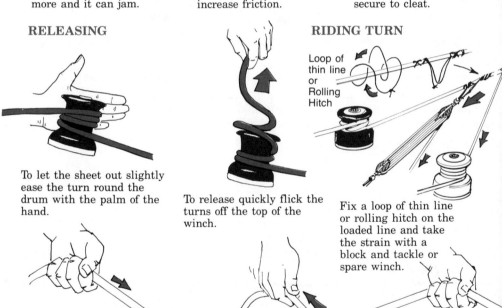

To let the sheet out slightly ease the turn round the drum with the palm of the hand.

To release quickly flick the turns off the top of the winch.

RIDING TURN

Loop of thin line or Rolling Hitch

Fix a loop of thin line or rolling hitch on the loaded line and take the strain with a block and tackle or spare winch.

EASING
Use the friction of one turn to ease a line underload.

SWIGGING (OR SWEATING)
To tighten a loaded line by pulling at right angles and snatching what you have gained around the cleat.

ROPE Throwing a rope is a skill worth practising. Coil the rope (page 15) and divide it into two. Swing and throw one coil underhand releasing the other coil as you do so.

MOORING ALONGSIDE

BOW (A) and STERNLINES (B) are needed to hold her in place, while BOW (C) and STERN SPRINGS (D) stop her sawing back and forth. (E) and (F) are BREAST ROPES which hold her against the quay but can often be left off. Guard against chafe where lines cross edges or each other. (G) is a FENDERBOARD used to span the piles on the quay.

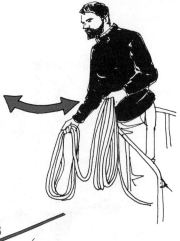

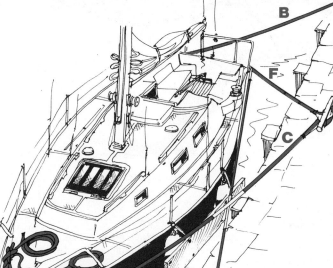

A round turn and two half hitches (H) is a good knot to use for mooring lines as it can be released under load.

If putting 'eyes' over a bollard (I) thread them through each other, so they can be released in any order.

ALLOWING FOR THE TIDE

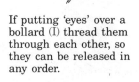

Try to use mooring lines at least 3 times as long as the rise of tide expected. Leave someone aboard to adjust fenders and lines if necessary.

21

SAFETY

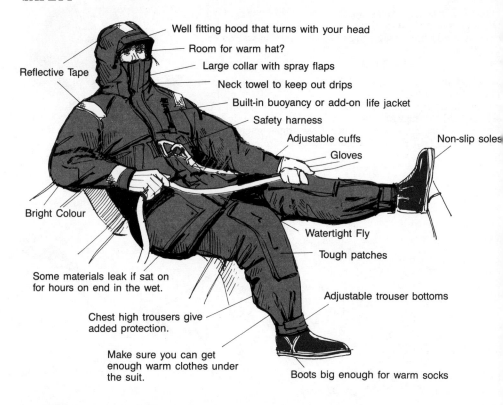

Well fitting hood that turns with your head

Room for warm hat?

Large collar with spray flaps

Neck towel to keep out drips

Built-in buoyancy or add-on life jacket

Safety harness

Adjustable cuffs

Gloves

Non-slip soles

Reflective Tape

Bright Colour

Some materials leak if sat on for hours on end in the wet.

Chest high trousers give added protection.

Make sure you can get enough warm clothes under the suit.

Watertight Fly

Tough patches

Adjustable trouser bottoms

Boots big enough for warm socks

SAFETY — Personal Equipment

Keeping warm and dry helps you stay alert and *SAFE*. So choose a good set of oilies that are *reall*
waterproof and check that the neck, cuff and ankle closures all adjust properly. Each member c
the crew must have a safety harness and life jacket.

DON'T FALL OVERBOARD

Hook on and sit down when working on deck

Hook on short so you can't go over the side

IF YOU DO GO OVER

A proper life jacket will let you maintain this 'survival' position which keeps you warm.

PRACTISE MAN OVERBOARD DRILL REGULARLY

22

SAFETY EQUIPMENT NEEDED

Bailing and Bilge Pumping
(A) Hand Bailers (B) Buckets with strong handles and lanyard (C) Bilge pumps.

Detection Equipment
(D) Radar reflector (E) Navigation lights (F) Foghorn (G) Powerful waterproof torch.

Fire Fighting Equipment
(H) Fire blanket (I) 2 Fire extinguishers (1.5 kg) Dry powder or (J) (1.5 kg) BCF (K) Automatic extinguisher for engine (see page 27).

Personal Safety Equipment
(L) Life jacket (M) Buoyancy aid (N) Safety harnesses (O) Liferaft

Man Overboard Equipment
(P) A dan buoy is easier to see than a person (Q) Life belt with (R) drogue and (S) self-igniting light (T) Boarding ladder

General Equipment
(U) Tender (V) Various warps for towing and mooring (W) Tools and spare parts (X) Emergency water supply (Y) Large fenders

A large first aid kit should also be carried and like all safety equipment *you should know how to use it*. Try to attend a course to practise using all the different types of safety gear you carry.

VHF RADIO DISTRESS CALL

A distress call is sent when there is *GRAVE AND IMMINENT* danger to a vessel or person and *IMMEDIATE ASSISTANCE* is required.

HOW TO SEND A DISTRESS CALL.

Switch on power, Switch on radio, *select CH16* Turn to high power Push press-to-transmit switch and speak slowly and distinctly.

Turning on the set etc. can be forgotten in an emergency so make up a reminder card and stick it up near the radio.

- MAYDAY, MAYDAY, MAYDAY.

MAYDAY is the international distress signal.

- This is (Yacht's Name 3 times)

- MAYDAY (Yacht's Name)

The 'name' and the word 'yacht' helps the searchers know what they are looking for. See below

- Position (see below)

- Nature of Distress

- Any extra information which might help

"I require immediate assistance" and include number of people on board, whether you are going to abandon ship or have fired flares etc.

- Over

'Over' means please reply.

AN URGENCY CALL

An urgency call is used when you have a *very important* message to send covering *safety.*

PAN PAN, PAN PAN, PAN PAN,
Hello all stations (3 times) this is (Yacht's name 3 times)
- Position
- Nature of Urgency
- Assistance Required
- Over

The advantage of an urgency call is that it lets the world know you are in some sort of trouble without launching all the rescue services at that moment.

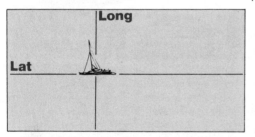

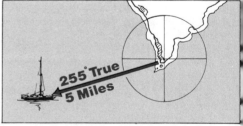

POSITIONS MUST BE GIVEN IN LAT. LONG. OR TRUE BEARINGS FROM A WELL DEFINED CHARTED POSITION WITH DISTANCE OFF. (e.g. Position 255° from South Head, 5 miles.)

If it is onboard, an Emergency Position Indicating Radio Beacon (or EPIRB) should be activated to raise the alarm and help the rescue services home in on you.

DISTRESS SIGNALS Marine pyrotechnics are a simple way of sending a distress signal. make sure *all* the crew know how to fire them. This is the *minimum* you should carry.

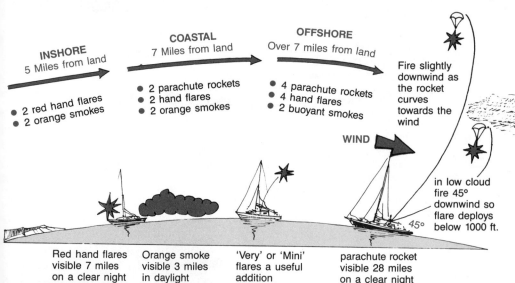

INSHORE
5 Miles from land

- 2 red hand flares
- 2 orange smokes

COASTAL
7 Miles from land

- 2 parachute rockets
- 2 hand flares
- 2 orange smokes

OFFSHORE
Over 7 miles from land

- 4 parachute rockets
- 4 hand flares
- 2 buoyant smokes

Fire slightly downwind as the rocket curves towards the wind

WIND

in low cloud fire 45° downwind so flare deploys below 1000 ft.

45°

Red hand flares visible 7 miles on a clear night

Orange smoke visible 3 miles in daylight

'Very' or 'Mini' flares a useful addition

parachute rocket visible 28 miles on a clear night

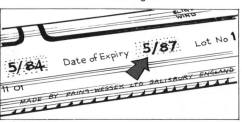

Always fire flares in groups of two as the first one might be missed by the person in charge of a potential rescue vessel.

Out of date flares do work but make sure there are always enough new ones onboard and inspect for signs of deterioration.

OTHER SIGNALS FOR HELP

Slowly raising and lowering your arms

A continuous sounding fog horn is a recognised distress signal.

A ball over or under a square shape works continuously and can be seen in poor light at long distances.

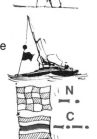

S.O.S. sent by any means

The signal NC can be made by flags or morse code

The signal 'V' means "I require assistance"
(not a distress signal)

LIFEBOAT While waiting for the lifeboat try to rig a bridle to spread the considerable towing loads over as many strong points as possible.

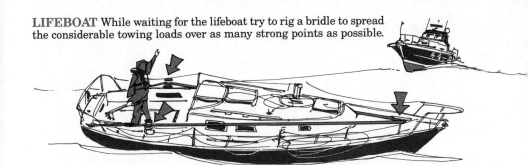

HELICOPTERS
DON'T — fire a flare near a helicopter (They'll lose night vision)
DON'T — touch the winch man in the air (you might get an electric shock!)
DON'T — attach the wire to the boat
DO — launch the liferaft if asked (to keep all clear of mast)
DO — take to the water in life jackets if asked (for the same reason)

LIFERAFTS
UNLESS THE BOAT IS SINKING FAST, OR ON FIRE, DON'T USE THE LIFERAFT.
You will stand more chance of being rescued, and suffer less from exposure in a flooded boat, than in a tiny liferaft.

Before launching all crew should put on warm clothes, oilskins and lifejackets. Also have ready *extra* emergency equipment eg. flares, EPIRB, water, food, space blankets.

The static line, once attached to the boat, might have to be pulled 25ft or more before inflation. Put a strong man in first for stability and to help weaker members aboard.

Cut the static line, stream the drogue to stop drift and add stability. Unplug the light during the day to save battery power.

Close main canopy, take seasick tablets, post a look-out, inflate double floor, tie in pump, spread out weight in rough weather or huddle together to keep warm.

THE RESCUERS ARE THE EXPERTS DO EXACTLY AS THEY SAY

FIRE
REMEMBER FIRE NEEDS:-
HEAT, FUEL AND *OXYGEN* CUT OUT ANY ONE AND THE FIRE GOES OUT.

CHECK BOAT FOR POTENTIAL FIRE HAZARDS — Such as:-
defective wiring, oil in bilge, accumulated waste paper or rags in lockers, suspect fuel or gas fittings.

NEVER smoke while refuelling or in a bunk.

ALWAYS turn the gas off at the bottle, 'earth' fuel filler pipes, fit flame traps on fuel tank vent pipes.

GAS HAZARDS Liquid petroleum gas is heavier than air so sinks into the bilges, if care is not taken. ALWAYS TURN OFF AT THE BOTTLE and let the gas burn out of the pipe. Then turn off at the stove. The bottle locker **MUST** drain overboard. A gas-detector is useful.

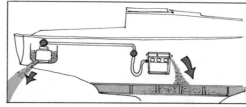

EXTINGUISHERS

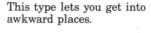

DRY POWDER
(Colour coded blue)
Best stowed on side so powder keeps getting shaken up.

HALON OR BCF
(Colour coded green)
Don't use any extinguisher on its side (to get under a door etc) as only half the gas or powder will come out.

This type lets you get into awkward places.

A small FIRE FIGHTING HOLE (A) is better than opening the engine box. An AUTOMATIC GAS TYPE (B) is best for this area.

DRY POWDER is very messy but does smother fire and stops reignition. Gas can fill awkward spaces but is toxic if breathed for long periods.

Don't forget water splashed from a bucket works better than tipping it on to a fire.

FIRE BLANKETS
FIRE BLANKETS (or wet dish cloths) can put out a galley fire. They are also essential for clothing fires —
- push the person over so flames rise away from face.
- Don't roll over, it spreads the fire
- Smother flames away from face with fire blanket or any suitable cloth.

RULE OF THE ROAD

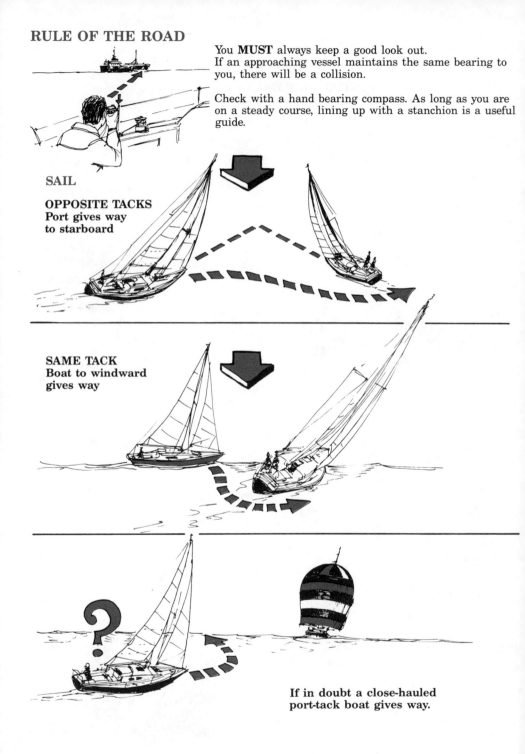

You **MUST** always keep a good look out.
If an approaching vessel maintains the same bearing to you, there will be a collision.

Check with a hand bearing compass. As long as you are on a steady course, lining up with a stanchion is a useful guide.

SAIL

OPPOSITE TACKS
Port gives way
to starboard

SAME TACK
Boat to windward
gives way

If in doubt a close-hauled
port-tack boat gives way.

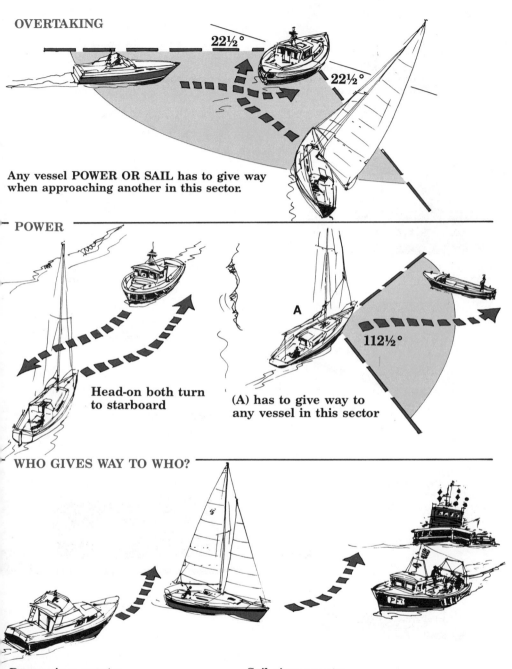

OVERTAKING

22½°

22½°

Any vessel **POWER OR SAIL** has to give way when approaching another in this sector.

POWER

Head-on both turn to starboard

A

112½°

(A) has to give way to any vessel in this sector

WHO GIVES WAY TO WHO?

Power gives way to:-
- sail
- vessel fishing
- vessel that can't manoeuvre

Sail gives way to:-
- vessel fishing
- vessel that can't manoeuvre

Ships are very large and often travelling very fast, so it makes sense to avoid a collision situation with one.

Far out at sea ships will normally give way to sailing boats but in confined waters they find evasive manoeuvres difficult and may be *"restricted in their ability to manoeuvre".*

From the bridge of a ship its hard to see even a large yacht and heavy rain or rough seas makes the radar screen confused as well.

If you decide he hasn't seen you, always make a *definite* change in course early to avoid confusion.

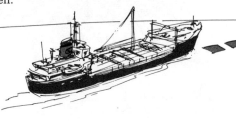

He *might* be altering course for another vessel over the horizon, which you can't even see yet! So be very careful.

What might seem a large expanse of water to us *is in fact a narrow channel* to a deep draught vessel. That's why small vessels must keep clear of large vessels in narrow channels.

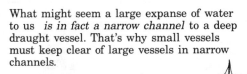

10 min

Travelling at *over 30 knots* today's ships can come from below the horizon to your position *in less than 10 minutes.*

SOUND SIGNALS

Every 2 minutes in bad visibility a power driven vessel (of any size) when under way will give *a long blast,* while a sailing vessel gives out *a long followed by two shorts.*

MANOEVRING SOUND SIGNALS

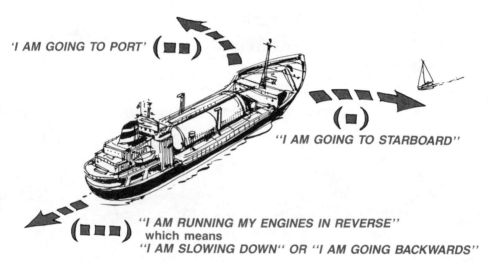

'I AM GOING TO PORT'

"I AM GOING TO STARBOARD"

"I AM RUNNING MY ENGINES IN REVERSE"
which means
"I AM SLOWING DOWN" OR "I AM GOING BACKWARDS"

WARNING SOUND SIGNALS

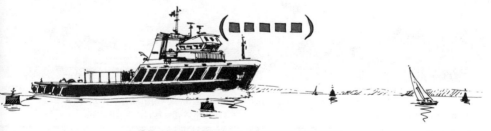

5 OR MORE SHORT BLASTS MEANS
"LOOK OUT-HAVE YOU SEEN ME!"

Warning sound signals are given when a vessel is unsure of the intentions of another, or doubts whether sufficient action has been taken by the other vessel to avoid a collision.

**For a complete list of regulations see RYA Booklet G2
"International Regulations for Preventing Collisions at Sea".**

LIGHTS

SIDELIGHTS   **MASTHEAD LIGHT**

Green 112.5°

Red 112.5°

White 225°   White 135°

STERN LIGHT

These are the lights that a yacht should show at night. The colours and cut-off angles give others a clue to what you are and the direction you are travelling in.

SAIL

POWER

POWER

Undersail a boat under 20 metres can show a combined RGW at the masthead.

Under power a white masthead light must show at least 1m above the RG sidelights.

A boat under 12m can show a white all round combined masthead and stern light when under power.

When sailing in rough seas a combined RGW masthead light is easier to see than one mounted lower down.

Yachts are even harder to see at night. Bright navigation marks and other ships lights over power the tiny yachts light in the foreground.

Ships lights can be lost against a background of shore lights. So take extra care when near the coast or entering harbour.

Fishing boats *special* lights can be lost in the blaze of deck lights. So, it is best to keep well clear of large fleets at night.

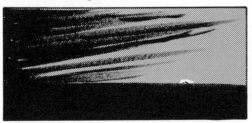

Beware of making the easy mistake of wrongly identifying a set of lights — this flood lit, slow moving, fishing boat way off on the horizon...

... could turn out to be an ocean liner ablaze with light travelling at over 30 knots which could be on top of you in a matter of minutes.

WHAT YOU SEE IN DAYLIGHT	WHAT YOU SEE AT NIGHT

AT ANCHOR MOTORSAILING

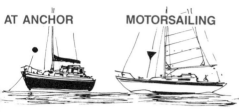

The relationship between a ships 2 white masthead lights shows which direction it is travelling.

The front masthead white light is the lower

FISHING

FISHING GEAR OUT 150M IN THIS DIRECTION

TRAWLING

PILOT VESSEL HOVERCRAFT

ALL ROUND FLASHING YELLOW LIGHT

TOWING VESSEL CANNOT MANOEUVRE

over 200m

RESTRICTED IN ABILITY TO MANOEUVRE BUT MAKING WAY.

MINE SWEEPING UNDER WATER WORK

SAFE SIDE DANGER SIDE

VESSEL CONSTRAINED BY HER DRAUGHT

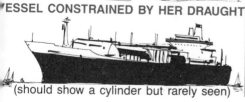

(should show a cylinder but rarely seen)

CHARTWORK Charts are overprinted with a lattice of latitude and longitude.

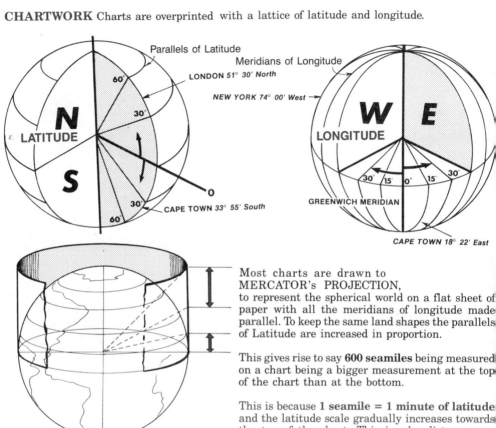

Parallels of Latitude

Meridians of Longitude

LONDON 51° 30′ North

NEW YORK 74° 00′ West →

N LATITUDE **S**

60°
30°
30°
60°

O

CAPE TOWN 33° 55′ South

W LONGITUDE **E**

30° 15° 0° 15° 30°

GREENWICH MERIDIAN

CAPE TOWN 18° 22′ East

Most charts are drawn to
MERCATOR's PROJECTION,
to represent the spherical world on a flat sheet of
paper with all the meridians of longitude made
parallel. To keep the same land shapes the parallels
of Latitude are increased in proportion.

This gives rise to say **600 seamiles** being measured
on a chart being a bigger measurement at the top
of the chart than at the bottom.

This is because **1 seamile = 1 minute of latitude**
and the latitude scale gradually increases towards
the top of the chart. *This is why distances are
ALWAYS* measured on the latitude scale opposite
your position.

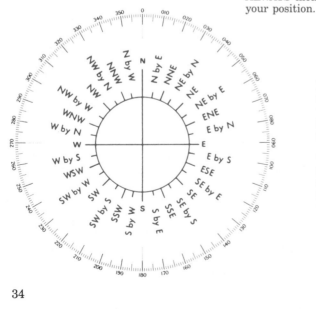

DIRECTION is always
measured from North in a
three figure notation **000°**
(North) 090° (East), 180°
(South) 270° (West) to 359°.

WIND DIRECTION is
usually in the form of points
of the compass ie. **N, NNE,**
NE by N etc.

PLOTTING A POSITION

A position on the earth's surface can be plotted in two ways:-

LATITUDE AND LONGITUDE say,
Latitude 45° 02' North by Longitude 5° 54' West
With a suitable instrument (see page 40) draw a line from 45° 02'N on the Latitude scale *up the side of the chart.*
Then mark off the position of 5° 54'W of Longitude.
One way to do this is to set your dividers from the nearest meridian to the position on the longitude scale *(top and bottom)* and transfer it to the 45° 02'N parallel.

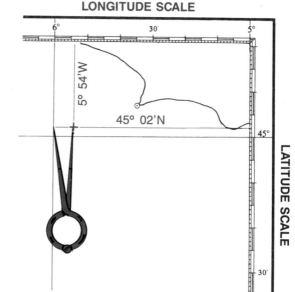

The other way of plotting a position is with a BEARING AND DISTANCE from a charted place.
Draw a line at the given bearing say 250° True from the charted place.
Transfer the bearing from the compass rose printed on the chart or use a suitable protractor (see page 40).
Then measure 15 minutes of latitude which equals 15 miles.
IT IS VERY IMPORTANT TO MEASURE FROM THE SCALE OPPOSITE YOUR POSITION (see page 34).
Step off the distance down your bearing line.

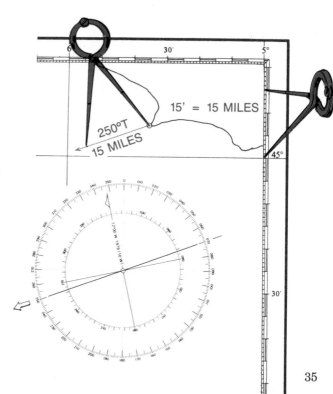

WHAT YOU SEE

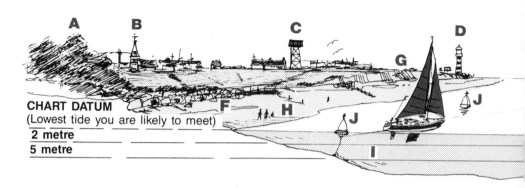

CHART DATUM
(Lowest tide you are likely to meet)

2 metre

5 metre

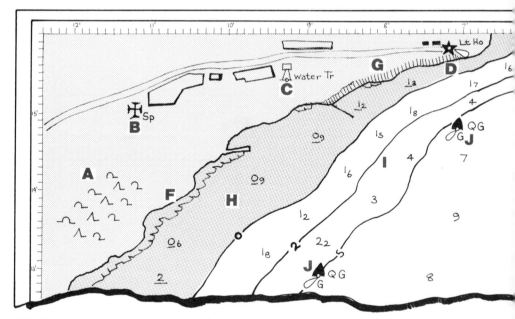

WHAT THE CHART SHOWS

Charts are just like land maps, using symbols to show useful features:- (A) — A MIXED WOOD
(B) — CHURCH WITH A SPIRE (C) — WATERTOWER (D) — LIGHTHOUSE (E) — LARGE
CHIMNEY (F) — ROCKY AREA (G) — CLIFFS.
Again like maps contour lines are shown but on charts it is the depth contours that are most useful.
The baseline or datum from which the depths are measured is based on the lowest tide you are
ever likely to meet. So with any tide you should have a bit more water than that shown on the
chart (see page 48-53) **but** where an area dries out H the height above chart datum is shown as
an underline number 1_2 mean 1.2 metres.

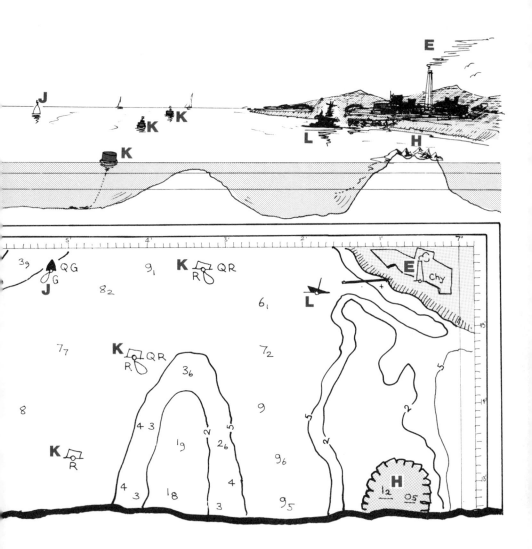

The depth or soundings are also measured in metres on modern charts and contour lines join similar depths together (I) Just like a contour line on a map, if the lines are close together, the bottom shelves steeply and if they are far apart there is a gentle slope. The navigation marks colour, lights and position are also plotted (J) STARBOARD HAND BUOYS (K) PORT HAND BUOYS so obviously the channel runs between them. Hazards such as WRECKS (L) are also shown together with details too numerous to list here.

Admiralty chart (actually a booklet) 5011
gives a complete list of chart symbols and abbreviations.

VARIATION is the angular difference between TRUE NORTH (top of world and top of chart) and MAGNETIC NORTH (what your compass should point at). As the magnetic field of the world is not constant, MAGNETIC NORTH gradually changes position.

This local VARIATION between TRUE AND MAGNETIC NORTH is shown on the compass rose printed on the chart.

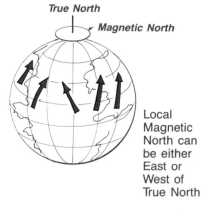

Local Magnetic North can be either East or West of True North

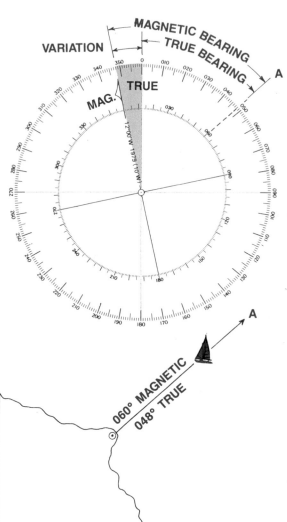

TRUE NORTH is pointing straight up while local variation was measured to be 12° WEST in 1979 *but decreasing* each year by 10' — so, in 1989 the VARIATION is only 10° 20' WEST.

Here we have a yacht off a well charted headland its MAGNETIC BEARING from the headland is 060° in 1979 and 58° 20' in 1989 but its TRUE BEARING is always 048°, no matter what year it is.

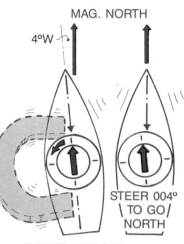

MAG. NORTH

4°W

STEER 004°
TO GO
NORTH

DEVIATION

Deviation is how far the magnetic influences of the boat pulls the compass needle away from Magnetic North. *Here it is pulled 4° West, so, to go North we need to steer 4° E.*

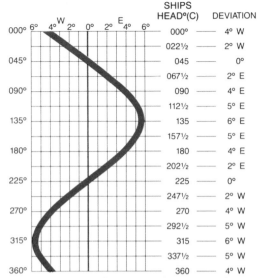

		W			E			SHIPS HEAD°(C)	DEVIATION
	6°	4°	2°	0°	2°	4°	6°		
000°								000°	4° W
								022½	2° W
045°								045	0°
								067½	2° E
090°								090	4° E
								112½	5° E
135°								135	6° E
								157½	5° E
180°								180	4° E
								202½	2° E
225°								225	0°
								247½	2° W
270°								270	4° W
								292½	5° W
315°								315	6° W
								337½	5° W
360°								360	4° W

If the compass does have deviation, then it needs to be checked on each heading and a **DEVIATION CURVE** like this drawn up.

COMPASS READS 067°

069°M

Every so often check the main compass by lining it up with a charted transit

COMPASS NEEDLE PULLED 2°E

To check the main ship's compass compare its reading with that of an accurate hand bearing compass that is being towed behind in a dinghy well away from all magnetic influences.

These can range from beer cans to large lumps of metal like the keel.

ERROR WEST = COMPASS BEST
4° W means compass must read 4° more
ERROR EAST = COMPASS LEAST
4° E means compass must read 4° less

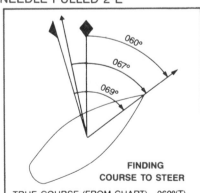

060°
067°
069°

**FINDING
COURSE TO STEER**

TRUE COURSE (FROM CHART)	060°(T)
VARIATION (FROM CHART)	9° W
MAGNETIC COURSE	069°(M)
DEVIATION (FROM TABLE)	2° E
COMPASS COURSE TO STEER	067°(C)

CHARTWORK

The instruments needed for chartwork are simply a soft pencil (2B), so you can rub out the lines easily, a pair of dividers to transfer measurements, and some means of measuring or transferring an angle.

Pencil and Dividers

A modern 'reloadable' pencil, saves a lot of mess and frustration when the sharpener goes missing! And a pair of brass dividers can be used single handed.

Parallel Rule

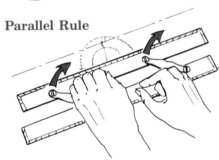

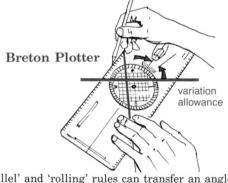

Breton Plotter

variation
allowance

Rolling Rule

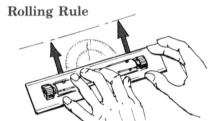

'Parallel' and 'rolling' rules can transfer an angle from the printed compass rose, by "walking" or rolling across the chart.

Rolling rules are good on dining room tables — almost useless on a yacht.

In rough conditions it is often easier to use a protractor of some sort. The Douglas protractor grid can be alined with the chart and the angle measured off. If working in "magnetic" you must make allowance for variation. With the 'Breton' and 'Hurst' plotters the protractor can be pre-set for variation.

This means when the grids are aligned with the chart the bearings read off are already in magnetic.

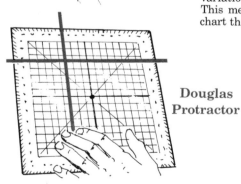

Douglas Protractor

Hurst Plotter

variation
allowance

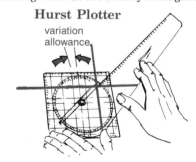

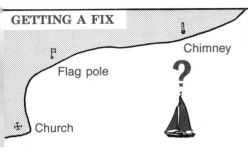

To find your position, you need 2 or preferably 3, charted objects.

Using a hand bearing compass, take each objects bearing in turn and note them

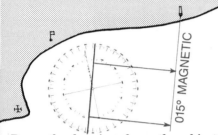

Draw the bearing from the object by either transferring the angle from the compass rose or by using a protractor.

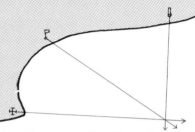

Do the same for the other 2 objects making sure you use the right bearing. Where the lines cross is your position.

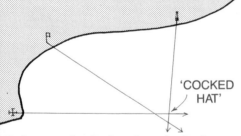

Unfortunately, the bearings don't always line up and so form a 'cocked hat'. Providing its not too big this is still OK.

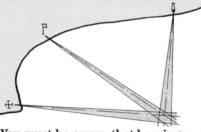

You must be aware that bearings can be slightly out, so mentally enlarge the area you are in for safety.

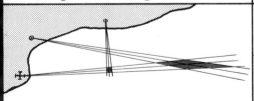

If, the objects are too close together, the area of uncertainty can enlarge dramatically. So, try to choose objects that will give 90° intesect.

Rough bearings can be taken on the edges of buildings or cliffs. Also by judging the centre of bays or the tops of mountains. Buoys are usually more accurate but they can be moved by storms.

WHAT THE TERMS MEAN ...

THE COURSE is the way we want to go and when related to the compass it is the COURSE TO STEER.

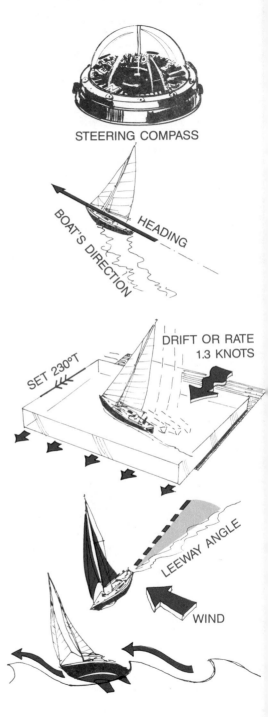

STEERING COMPASS

THE HEADING is the way the boat is pointing, ideally this should be the same as the course. If not, the helmsman must note in the log the course actually steered.

Note the boat is moving through the water in a different direction from the heading this is due LEEWAY.

TIDAL SET AND DRIFT
SET is the direction the tide is going and DRIFT is the distance the water has moved in a period of time.
(If the water has drifted say 1.3 miles in 1 hour it's called a RATE of 1.3 KNOTS).

Symbol to draw on chart

LEEWAY is how much we are blown sideways by the wind. Measuring the bearing of the wake and comparing it with the reciprocal of the HEADING gives us a clue. But this is only possible in calm conditions and most people estimate say 3°5° based on past experience.
In rough condition 10°20° of LEEWAY is possible as the boat can be bodily moved sideways.

WATER TRACK is the path we make through the water (ie the wake) allowing to leeway.

Symbol to draw on chart

GROUND TRACK is the actual path we make over the sea bed.

Symbol to draw on chart

DEAD RECKONING (D.R.) is a position deduced from a course steered and a distance run. *It makes no allowance for tidal set and drift or leeway* so is of little practical use in coastal navigation.

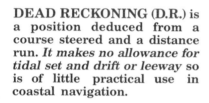

ESTIMATED POSITION (E.P.) is the best possible estimate of a present or future position. It is based on a distance run from a known position *with an allowance made for both leeway and the tidal set and drift.*

Symbol △

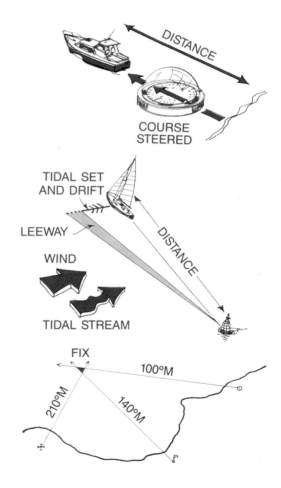

A FIX is when we know where we are by using compass, radio direction bearings, depth soundings, transits or one of the many electronic aids to navigation available now.

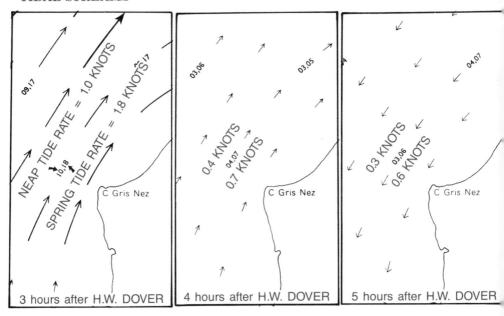

3 hours after H.W. DOVER | 4 hours after H.W. DOVER | 5 hours after H.W. DOVER

The *rate* and *direction* of tidal streams can be depicted in different ways:-

THE TIDAL STREAM ATLAS (above), by using a separate page for each hour either side of high water at a *standard port*, gives a more graphic display. So you can see at a glance when the tide turns but you must use a protractor to measure its direction

THE TIDAL DIAMONDS (below) on the chart do the same job but the direction is given as a *TRUE BEARING*. The strength or *RATE* for the hour in both cases, has to be estimated if you are between *SPRING* AND *NEAP* tides (see page 48).

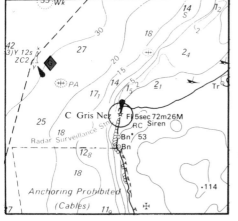

	Hours	Dir	Rate(kn) Sp	Rate(kn) Np	Dir	Rate(kn) Sp	Rate(kn) Np	Dir	Rate(kn) Sp	Rate(kn) Np	Dir
After H	3	248	1·8		031	1·2	0·6	054	0·5		·31
	4	248	1·7	1·0	031	0·4	0·2	S l	a c	k	S
	5	248	1·6	0·9	211	0·4	0·2	219	0·4	0·2	203
	6	249	1·2	0·7	211	1·3	0·7	217	0·8	0·4	210
		(F) 50°58·6N 1 26·8E			(G) 50°53·5N 1 31·5E			(H) 50°42·0N 1 25·0E			(I) 50
Before HW	6	206	1·7	1·0	214	2·5	1·4	201	1·5	0·8	214
	5	204	2·5	1·4	209	3·3	1·9	200	2·0	1·1	213
	4	208	2·7	1·5	208	3·2	1·8	194	2·1	1·2	203
	3	209	2·1	1·2	205	2·1	1·2	174	1·2	0·7	152
	2	221	0·9	0·5	183	0·4	0·1	076	0·5	0·3	040
	1	017	0·7	0·4	029	1·6	0·9	019	1·0	0·6	032
	HW	026	2·0	1·1	026	3·2	1·8	007	1·7	1·0	028
After HW	1	028	2·6	1·5	025	3·6	2·0	011	2·0	1·1	022
	2	030	2·4	1·4	028	2·5	1·4	014	1·6	0·9	026
	3	033	1·7	0·9	027	1·8	1·0	012	0·8	0·4	335
	4	028	0·6	0·3	030	0·7	0·4	337	0·1	0·0	236
	5	214	0·4	0·2	205	0·6	0·3	204	0·6	0·3	209
	6	209	1·4	0·8	213	1·9	1·1	200	1·2	0·7	213

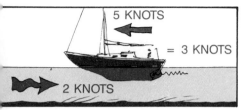

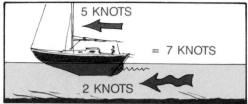

The tidal stream can either hold you back or try to to push you along. When it comes from the side its like crossing a river. If there was no tidal stream we could cross from A to B in a straight line but when the stream pushes on the side of the boat we end up at C.

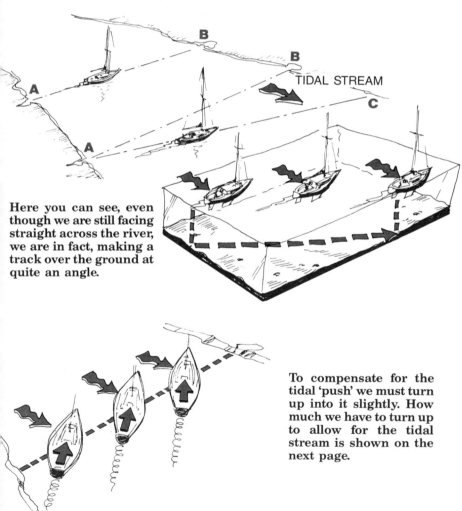

Here you can see, even though we are still facing straight across the river, we are in fact, making a track over the ground at quite an angle.

To compensate for the tidal 'push' we must turn up into it slightly. How much we have to turn up to allow for the tidal stream is shown on the next page.

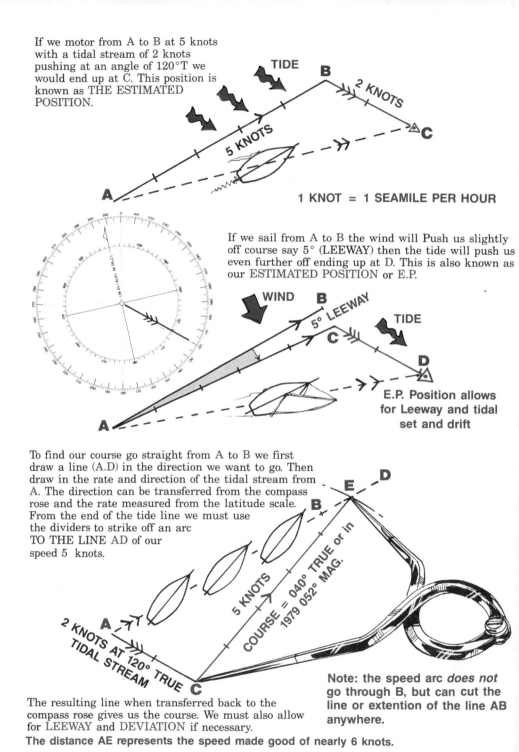

If we motor from A to B at 5 knots with a tidal stream of 2 knots pushing at an angle of 120°T we would end up at C. This position is known as THE ESTIMATED POSITION.

TIDE

B

2 KNOTS

C

5 KNOTS

A

1 KNOT = 1 SEAMILE PER HOUR

If we sail from A to B the wind will Push us slightly off course say 5° (LEEWAY) then the tide will push us even further off ending up at D. This is also known as our ESTIMATED POSITION or E.P.

WIND **B** **5° LEEWAY** **TIDE**

C

D

A

E.P. Position allows for Leeway and tidal set and drift

To find our course go straight from A to B we first draw a line (A.D) in the direction we want to go. Then draw in the rate and direction of the tidal stream from A. The direction can be transferred from the compass rose and the rate measured from the latitude scale. From the end of the tide line we must use the dividers to strike off an arc TO THE LINE AD of our speed 5 knots.

D

E

B

5 KNOTS

COURSE = 040° TRUE or in 1979 052° MAG.

A

2 KNOTS AT 120° TRUE TIDAL STREAM

C

The resulting line when transferred back to the compass rose gives us the course. We must also allow for LEEWAY and DEVIATION if necessary.

Note: the speed arc *does not* go through B, but can cut the line or extention of the line AB anywhere.

The distance AE represents the speed made good of nearly 6 knots.

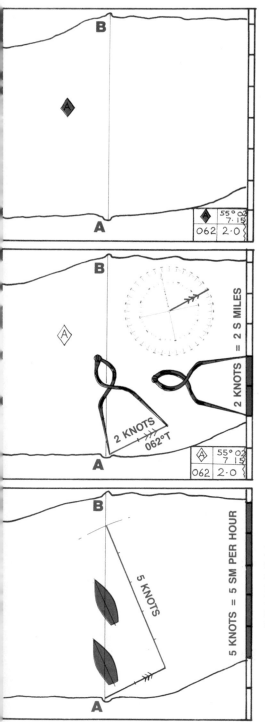

To go from A to B we find the nearest *tidal diamond* and check the *rate and direction* for the time we are travelling. That means the time in relation to the time of high water at the Standard Port.

We transfer the *true bearing of 062°* from the compass rose to our starting point and as we have a SPRING TIDE we can use the figure of **2 KNOTS.** We measure **2 miles** from the scale at the edge of the chart opposite our position.
ANY LINE DRAWN TO SCALE SHOWING A BEARING AND A SPEED IS KNOWN AS A 'VECTOR'.

From the end of the tidal vector we strike off an arc equal to the speed we hope to average on the trip, say **5 KNOTS.** Where the arc cuts the line AB we draw a line which is our course. If we transfer this line back to the compass rose we get our course to steer. Again if there is any cross wind we must allow for leeway.

TIDES

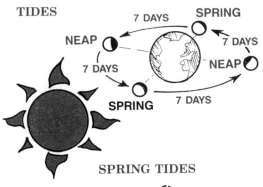

The gravitational 'pulls' of the SUN and the MOON control the tides. When the sun and moon are in line they form SPRING TIDES and when they are at right angles they form NEAP TIDES. As you can see this changes roughly every 7 days as it takes about 28 days for the moon to orbit the earth.

SPRING TIDES

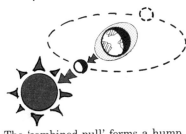

The 'combined pull' forms a hump of water which causes very high and very low levels of high and low water.

NEAP TIDES

The 'offset pull' forms a more moderate change in the levels of high and low water.

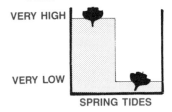

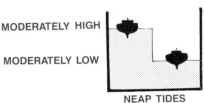

A high water 'hump' is formed on both sides of the world. So, every day we spin through two high water levels and two low water levels. A large 'hump' of water (SPRINGS) moving between land masses causes strong tidal streams, while small 'humps' (NEAPS) cause weaker tidal streams.

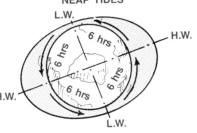

VERY STRONG WINDS CAN 'HOLD' THE 'TIDE IN' OR PUSH THE 'TIDE OUT'

Unfortunately WIND and AIR PRESSURE can cause fluctuations in predicted levels.

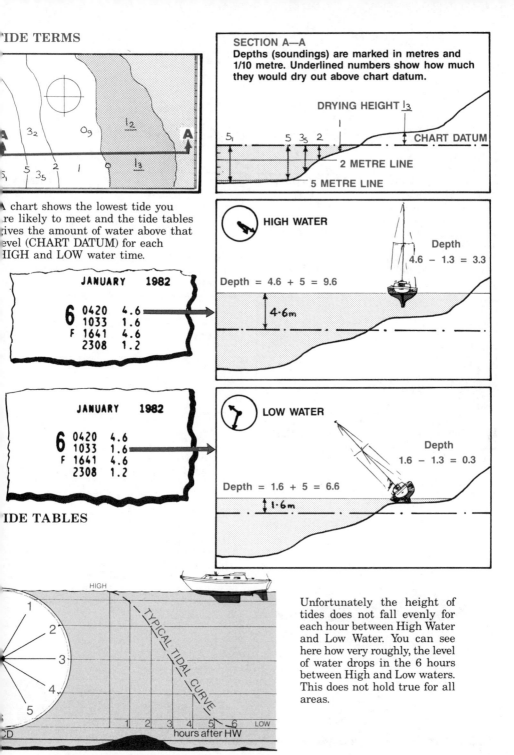

TIDE TERMS

3_2 0_9 $|_2$
5_1 3_5 2 $|$ 0 $|_3$

SECTION A—A
Depths (soundings) are marked in metres and
1/10 metre. Underlined numbers show how much
they would dry out above chart datum.

DRYING HEIGHT $|_3$
CHART DATUM
5_1 5 3_5 2 $|$
2 METRE LINE
5 METRE LINE

A chart shows the lowest tide you
are likely to meet and the tide tables
gives the amount of water above that
level (CHART DATUM) for each
HIGH and LOW water time.

JANUARY 1982

6 0420 4.6
1033 1.6
F 1641 4.6
2308 1.2

HIGH WATER

Depth = 4.6 + 5 = 9.6

4·6m

Depth
4.6 − 1.3 = 3.3

JANUARY 1982

6 0420 4.6
1033 1.6
F 1641 4.6
2308 1.2

TIDE TABLES

LOW WATER

Depth = 1.6 + 5 = 6.6

1·6m

Depth
1.6 − 1.3 = 0.3

HIGH

TYPICAL TIDAL CURVE

1 2 3 4 5 6

1 2 3 4 5 6 LOW
hours after HW

Unfortunately the height of
tides does not fall evenly for
each hour between High Water
and Low Water. You can see
here how very roughly, the level
of water drops in the 6 hours
between High and Low waters.
This does not hold true for all
areas.

TIDAL TERMS

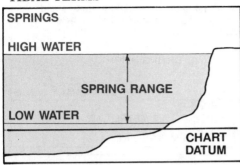

SPRINGS

HIGH WATER

SPRING RANGE

LOW WATER

CHART DATUM

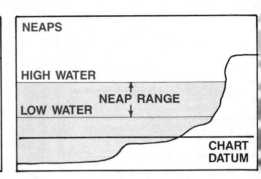

NEAPS

HIGH WATER

NEAP RANGE

LOW WATER

CHART DATUM

Mean High Water Springs M.H.W.S.
is the average height of all the SPRING HIGH WATERS.
Mean Low Water Springs M.L.W.S.
is the average height of all the SPRING LOW WATERS.

Mean High Water Neaps M.H.W.N.
is the average height of all the NEAP HIGH WATERS.
Mean Low Water Neaps M.L.W.N.
is the average height of all the NEAP LOW WATERS.

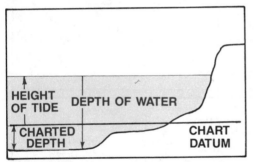

HEIGHT OF TIDE   DEPTH OF WATER

CHARTED DEPTH

CHART DATUM

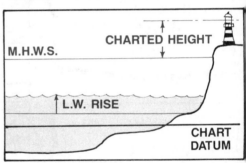

CHARTED HEIGHT

M.H.W.S.

L.W. RISE

CHART DATUM

Height of tide is always measured from the CHART DATUM (lowest tide you are likely to meet)**Depths of Water** are measured from the HEIGHT to the sea bed. **Charted depth** is measured from CHART DATUM to sea bed.

Charted Heights, such as heights of lights or clearance under bridges, are always measured from M.H.W.S (The highest average tide height) **Rise of tide** is how much the water has risen from L.W. for that day.

MEASURING THE DEPTH
The depth of water can be measured with an echo-sounder. This measures the time differences between transmitted and reflected signals and converts them into depth readings. An allowance has to be made for the depth of the transducer in the hull and the keel.

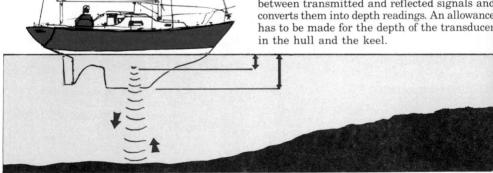

USING TIDAL HEIGHT CALCULATIONS

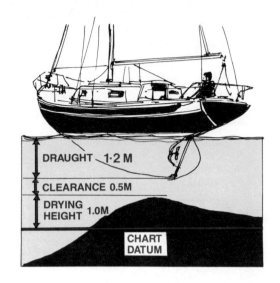

What height of tide is needed to cross a sand bank with a charted drying height of 1.0m in a boat which draws 1.2m, with a clearance of 0.5m under the keel?

Height of tide needed is:-
Draught + clearance + drying height
= 1.2 + 0.5 + 1.0
= 2.7m

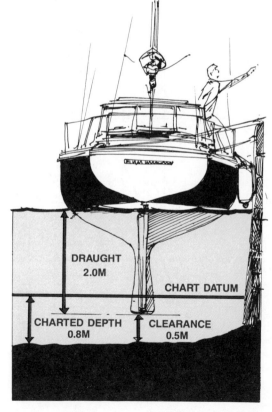

What height of tide will be needed to go alongside in a berth where the charted depth is 0.8m in a boat drawing 2.0m with 0.5 clearance under the keel?

Height of tide needed is:-
Draught + clearance −
charted depth
= 2.0 + 0.5 − 0.8
= 1.7m

TIDAL CURVES provide a means of finding the height of tide between high and low water. *Example: At what time will there be 8 metres of water in St. Helier on 8th June?*

CHANNEL ISLANDS - ST. HELIER
LAT 49°11'N   LONG 2°07'W
TIMES AND HEIGHTS OF HIGH AND LOW WATERS

JUNE

M	TIME	M		TIME	M		TIME	M	
.55	8.7	**7**	0158	8.5	**22**	0314	8.9	**7**	0159 F
.42	3.3		0833	3.7		0953	3.1		0839
.37	8.7	SU	1436	8.6	M	1542	8.9	TU	1443
:17	3.4					2220	3.1		2114
.00	1	**8**	0256	8.9	**23**	04 7	9.1	**8**	0310
.45	8		0932	3.2		10	3.0		0948
.34	2	M	1529	9.2	TU	15 1	9.2	W	1548
12	9		2157	3.0		08	2.9		2220
53	9.6	**9**	1026	2.7	**24**	0458	9.2	**9**	0417 1
35	2.4					1129	2.8		1052 2
20	9.6	TU	1619	9.8	W	1716	9.4	TH	1649 9
59	2.4		2251	2.5		2354	2.7		2325 ;

1. Refer to the tide table for 8th June.

2. Find the tidal curve for St. Helier (Nautical Almanacs).

3. Write in the H.W. time and fill in the boxes for each hour before H.W. (Rounding up or down) until you reach L.W. time.

4. Mark in the heights of H.W. and L.W.

5. Join the 9.2 to 3.2 with a line AB.

6. Find the 8 metre mark and drop a line until it hits AB.

7. Go horizontally until you reach the relevant curve for Springs or Neaps then drop down to find the time.

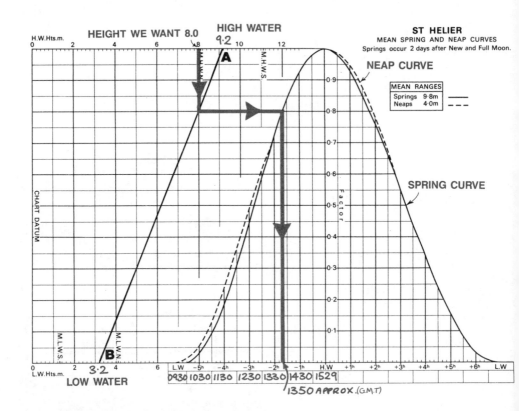

You can also find what height of tide there will be at a specific time by working backwards from the time scale ie. *How much water at 13.50?*. Go up to the curve, then horizontal to the line and up to the top scale = 8 metres.

SECONDARY PORTS

Nautical Almanacs publish the tidal height and time differences between large (STANDARD) ports and small (SECONDARY) ports.

ST HELIER	TIME DIFFERENCES				HEIGHT DIFF.			
	HIGH WATER		LOW WATER		MHWS	MHWN	MLWN	MLWS
	0300	0900	0200	0900	11.1	8.1	4.1	1.3
	1500	2100	1400	2100				
BRAYE	+0050	+0040	+0025	+0105	-4.8	-3.4	-1.5	-0.5

So, if H.W. is at 0300 or 1500 it will be 50 mins later at BRAYE
But, if H.W. is at 0900 or 2100 it will be 40 mins later at BRAYE
Also when there is 11.1 metres at H.W. at St. Helier then will be 4.8 metres less at BRAYE etc.

However, if high and low water falls between these set times, we must interpolate (estimate) between the "difference" figures. This can be done by eye but a graph is more accurate.

ST. HELIER time	height (m)
1647	3.2 L.W.
2233	9.2 H.W.

What time and height is low water at BRAYE?

Low Water BRAYE:- Time = 16.47 + 0040 = 17.27 GMT.
Height = 3.2 - 1.2 = 2 metres.

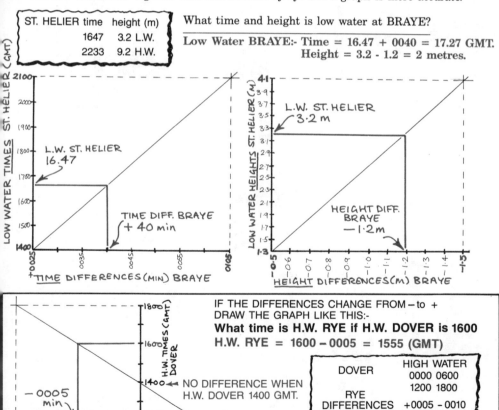

IF THE DIFFERENCES CHANGE FROM – to +
DRAW THE GRAPH LIKE THIS:-
What time is H.W. RYE if H.W. DOVER is 1600
H.W. RYE = 1600 – 0005 = 1555 (GMT)

NO DIFFERENCE WHEN
H.W. DOVER 1400 GMT.

	HIGH WATER
DOVER	0000 0600
	1200 1800
RYE DIFFERENCES	+0005 – 0010

REMEMBER THESE ARE ALL APPROXIMATE SO ALWAYS ALLOW AN ADEQUATE SAFETY MARGIN

BUOYAGE

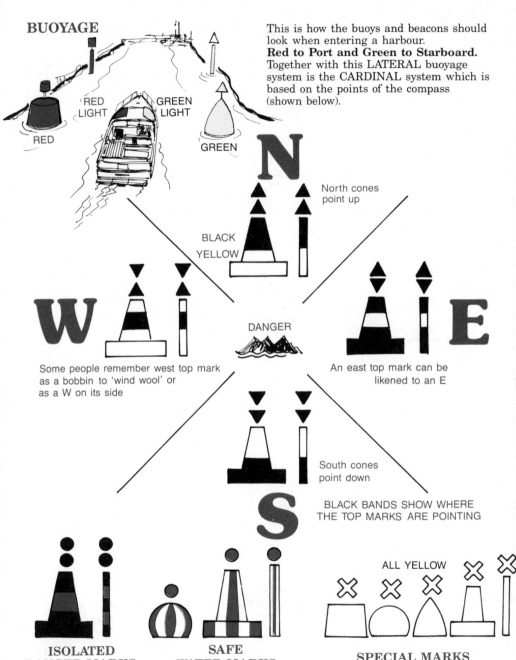

This is how the buoys and beacons should look when entering a harbour.
Red to Port and Green to Starboard.
Together with this LATERAL buoyage system is the CARDINAL system which is based on the points of the compass (shown below).

RED LIGHT

GREEN LIGHT

RED

GREEN

N

North cones point up

BLACK

YELLOW

W

Some people remember west top mark as a bobbin to 'wind wool' or as a W on its side

DANGER

E

An east top mark can be likened to an E

S

South cones point down

BLACK BANDS SHOW WHERE THE TOP MARKS ARE POINTING

ISOLATED DANGER MARKS

Danger with safe water all around.

LIGHT: WHITE GP FL (2)

SAFE WATER MARKS

Safe deep water
LIGHT WHITE
ISOPHASE, OCCULTING
LONG FLASH
OR MORE 'A'

SPECIAL MARKS

ALL YELLOW

Special marks can mean: anything from a deep channel to a swimming area (See char for details).

LIGHT YELLOW (SEE CHART FOR DETAILS)

54

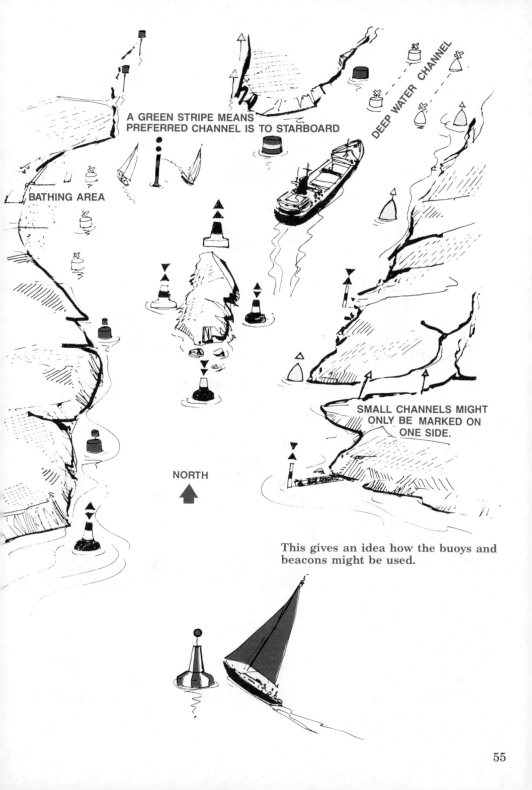

A GREEN STRIPE MEANS
PREFERRED CHANNEL IS TO STARBOARD

DEEP WATER CHANNEL

BATHING AREA

SMALL CHANNELS MIGHT
ONLY BE MARKED ON
ONE SIDE.

NORTH

This gives an idea how the buoys and
beacons might be used.

BUOYAGE

Buoys vary in size and construction. They often sport strange shaped radar reflectors, light platforms and solar or wind generators. Many have no top marks at all just a plain red or green buoy and in small channels there may only be a painted stick! Port and Starboard buoys have red or green lights but cardinal marks flash white, as below like the numbers on a clock.

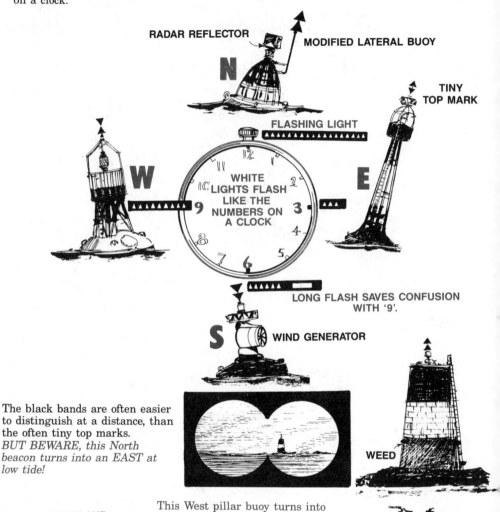

RADAR REFLECTOR

MODIFIED LATERAL BUOY

N

TINY TOP MARK

FLASHING LIGHT

W

WHITE LIGHTS FLASH LIKE THE NUMBERS ON A CLOCK

E

9   **3**

LONG FLASH SAVES CONFUSION WITH '9'.

S   WIND GENERATOR

The black bands are often easier to distinguish at a distance, than the often tiny top marks.
BUT BEWARE, this North beacon turns into an EAST at low tide!

WEED

QUICK AND VERY QUICK FLASHING

This West pillar buoy turns into a South in a strong tidal stream.

New uncharted wrecks often have double buoys around them.

Roosting birds and their 'guando' have turned this N into a W.

LIGHTS

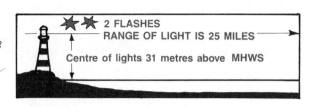

The abbreviations for lights are explained fully in (Admiralty booklet 5011), but this is what BEACHY HEAD is like.

F1 (2) 20 sec = 2 flashes every 20 secs.
31m = 31 metres above MHWS
25m = 25 mile range in good weather
Explos. = Explosive fog signal

SECTOR LIGHTS

Some lights have coloured sectors to indicated special navigational problems. Sometimes to show where the channel is — so if you stray to port you see red and if you stray to starboard you see green. Or, they can be used to cover a dangerous area but the chart or pilot book will give details.

LEADING LIGHTS

Harbour entrances are sometimes marked with 'leading lights'. When the lights line up you are in the channel. When they do not you can see which way to steer. The lower light is always in front.

LIGHT CHARACTERISTICS

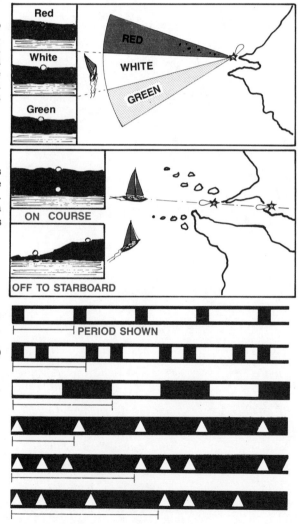

Occulting (Oc) single more light than dark

Group occulting Oc (2)

Isophase (equal light & dark) Iso.

Single flashing F1.

Group flashing F1 (3)

Composite group flashing F1 (2 + 1)

PILOTAGE

Pilotage is the skill of navigating in confined waters. There will seldom be time to plot fixes and EP's so you need to use other means to keep track of your position and course to steer.

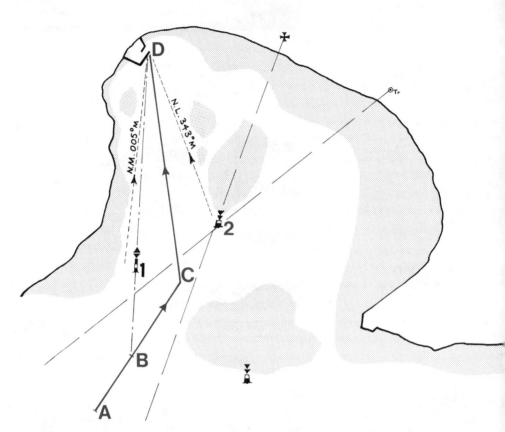

Pre-planning is essential:-

FROM A —   Bn2 bears 018°(M). This gives a leading line through the shoal.

AT B —   The breakwater is in transit with Bn1 and should bear 001°(M). This will give a positive identification of the breakwater end.

BETWEEN A & C — Clearing transits are available in case you have to leave the plotted track.

AT C —   Alter course when breakwater end bears 355°(M) to steer towards it.

BETWEEN C & D — Clearing bearings on breakwater end. (No Less (N.L.) than 343°, No More (N.M.) than 005°.)

SOUNDINGS —   Watch the echo sounder it will warn you if you are going the wrong way.

Beware of seeing "what you want to see"! The charted WHITE BUILDINGS, you have been looking for are there dead on course

BUT through the binoculars, turn out to be a brand new caravan site! This is a very easy mistake to make especially when you are tired.

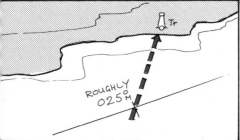

ROUGHLY 025°M

As it is not always easy to identify the landmark you are looking for check by measuring a rough bearing from your charted position.

Then go on deck and swing your handbearing compass onto that bearing. By looking near the bearing you should see the landmark you want.

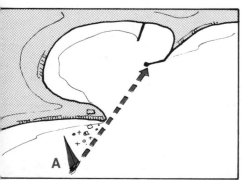

A

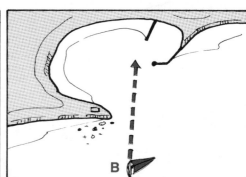

B

VIEW FROM A — BAY 'CLOSED'

From the chart we see that if the cliff and the end of the harbour wall line up we will be too close to the rocks.

VIEW FROM B — BAY 'OPEN'

So, provided the cliffs and the end of the harbour wall remain separated, or 'open' we will be in safe water.

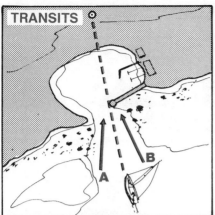

TRANSITS

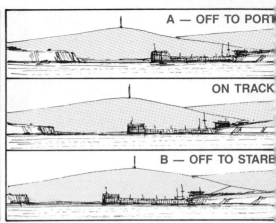

A — OFF TO PORT

ON TRACK

B — OFF TO STARB

We are on course for the harbour when the end of the seawall and the beacon are in line. This is known as a transit.

So, when we are off track to port we shall see view (A) and if we are off track to starboard we shall see view (B).

TRANSIT PLUS BEARING

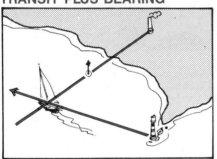

Transits can be found by lining up anything on the chart, like the edge of a building or breakwater, here we have a beacon and chimney.

The transit coupled with a bearing gives us a very good fix. The bearing of the lighthouse is taken when the the beacon and chimney are in line and it is transferred to the chart.

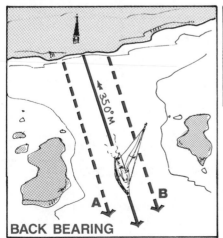

BACK BEARING

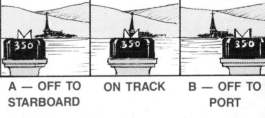

A — OFF TO STARBOARD

ON TRACK

B — OFF TO PORT

If the only available landmark is astern we shall need to take a back bearing, to see if we are off track. This can sometimes be awkward to work out so often it is easier to see what the correct bearing should be from the chart. Then set the hand bearing compass to it and see if we are to port of starboard of the desired line.

CLEARING LINES

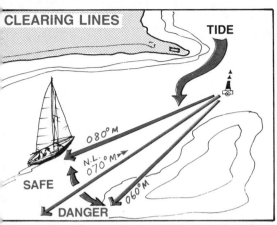

Here we have drawn a line at 070° mangetic to the North cardinal buoy. Provided our hand bearing compass always reads *more* than 070° we shall be clear of the shallow water. *N.L. (not less) 070°M.*

IN SAFE WATER

IN SHALLOW WATER!

This is what we might see:-
080° Magnetic is fine but if we get swept in by the tide until it read 060°M we are in trouble!

TWO CLEARING LINES

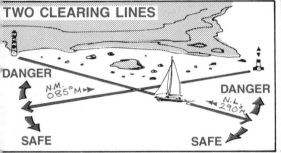

We can use two clearing bearings to sail around a potential hazard on our course. Over the stern 085° or *more* means trouble. While over the bow 290° or *less* is dangerous.

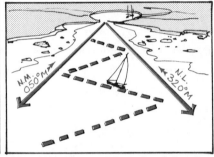

These bearings can be used to define the maximum area we can tack in. Any *lower* than 320° and any higher than 050° means trouble.

TURNING POINTS

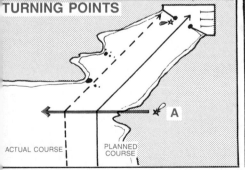

Here we have chosen to turn on to a new course when light (A) is abeam. But if we have been set slightly out say on to the dotted line we shall end up on the rocks.

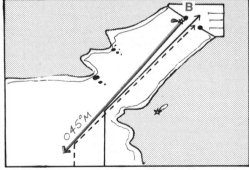

Much better to choose a turning point to align more closely to our new course. Say when light (B) bears 045°M then any error will be smaller and less dramatic!

PASSAGE PLANNING

A SKIPPERS CHECKLIST such as this should be completed before leaving harbour:

- Probable destination — approximate distance.
- Viable alternatives — approximate distance.
- Ports of refuge — entry criteria.
- Weather forecast.
- Times of High Water at reference port(s) — B.S.T.
- Critical points of Tidal 'Gates' on passage.
- Times of favourable tides.
- Times of adverse tides.
- Critical heights and times of tides required to:
  a) Leave b) Cross Bars etc., c) Enter Harbours
- Dangers en route (clearing lines, safe distance off etc.,)
- List of lights, buoys, navigational features.
- Approximate courses to make good on chart, with distance and landmarks.
- Strategy.
- Publications for Pilotage information.
- Prepare detailed Pilotage plan for unfamiliar harbours.
- Correct charts available.
- Food prepared, boat victualled.

FOG

UNDER SAIL

UNDER POWER

If fog is approaching:-
- Check where you are by taking bearings
- Hoist the radar reflector (correct attitude if not permanently rigged)
- Put on life jacket and maybe even tow the dinghy (in case you are run down)
- Post look-outs to 'listen and look' (Turn off engine occasionally)
- Try to keep out of shipping lanes by heading for shallow water
- Use your foghorn every 2 minutes
- Use every electronic device you have to maintain good position on the chart.

WEATHER

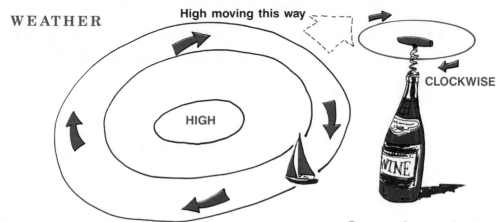

High moving this way

HIGH

CLOCKWISE

In the Northern hemisphere, air circulates in a *clockwise* direction in a **HIGH** (anticyclone) so, as it passes North of the yacht the wind will change from North to East.

Some people remember the direction by:- HIGH = GOOD WEATHER So, open a bottle of wine, CLOCKWISE, WITH A CORK SCREW!

ISOBARS are contour lines joining places of equal air pressure

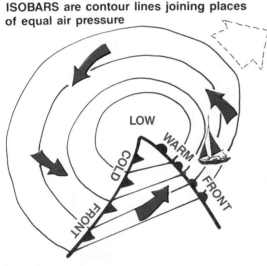

LOW

COLD FRONT

WARM FRONT

ANTI-CLOCKWISE

In a **LOW** pressure system (Depression or Cyclone) the air goes around *anti-clockwise*. Therefore the yacht feels the wind change from South East to South West as the LOW passes to the North.

Likewise, in a LOW there is often BAD WEATHER so, open the whisky bottle ANTI-CLOCKWISE.

As a **WARM FRONT** passes over us the wind will change direction often increasing in strength. The heavy rain should decrease and visibility will deteriorate with possible fog.

But, as the **COLD FRONT** passes over the wind will again change direction after with squalls. The heavy rain will give way to clearer weather with the visibility improving.

WEATHER FORECASTS

These are available on local radio, television, V.H.F. radio or by telephoning a special number. National newspapers publish weather maps and a 'NAVTEX' teleprinter service can also be fitted to your boat. The most common source of weather information is the BBC shipping forecasts which are broadcast at set times each day on the Radio.

To save time these bulletins follow a set pattern and use standard terms.

The general synopsis — How and where the pressure systems are moving.

Sea area forecasts —
Each area follows the same pattern.
● WIND — Direction and strength
● WEATHER — Rain etc
● VISIBILITY — Good, moderate poor

Coastal Station
Reports:-
● WIND
● SIGNIFICANT WEATHER
● VISIBILITY in miles or metres
● Pressure in millibars
● Pressure tendancy 'rising' or 'falling'

MEANINGS OF TERMS USED IN WEATHER FORECASTS

GALE WARNINGS: If the average wind is expected to increase to F8 or more, or gust of 43kn are expected. SEVERE GALES if the wind is expected to increase to F9 (41kn) or over, or gusts of 52kn are expected.

STORMS: if the average wind is expected to increase to F10 (48kn) or over, or gusts of 61kn are expected.

IMMINENT: within 6 hours from time of issue of the warning.

SOON: between 6-12 hours from time of issue of the warning.

LATER: after 12 hours from time of issue.

WIND STRENGTHS: Land forecasts use the following: Calm = 0; Light = F1-3; Moderate = F4; Fresh = F5; Strong = F6-7; Gale = F8.

VISIBILITY: descriptions of visibility in shipping forecasts mean the following:
Good: more than 5nM
Moderate: 2-5nM
Poor: 1,100yds to 2nM
Fog: less than 1,100yds

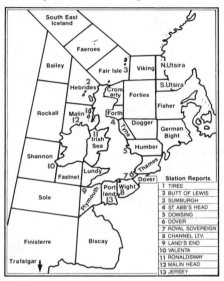

Station Reports.	
1	TIREE
2	BUTT OF LEWIS
3	SUMBURGH
4	ST ABB'S HEAD
5	DOWSING
6	DOVER
7	ROYAL SOVEREIGN
8	CHANNEL LT.V.
9	LAND'S END
10	VALENTA
11	RONALDSWAY
12	MALIN HEAD
13	JERSEY

Coastal station reports use the following:
Mist or haze: 1,100-2,200 yds
Fog: less than 1,100yds

FAIR: used when there is nothing significant. ie. no showers, mist, rain, etc.

PRESSURE and TENDANCY:
Steady: Change less than 0.1mb in 3 hrs
Rising or Falling Slowly: Change 0.1 to 1.5mb in last 3 hrs.
Rising or Falling: Change 1.6 to 3.5mb in last 3 hrs.
Rising or Falling Quickly: Change 3.6 to 6.0mb in last 3 hrs.
Rising or Falling Very Rapidly: Change of more than 6.0mb in last 3 hrs.
Now Falling, now rising:Change from rising to falling or vice versa within last 3 hours.

PRESSURE SYSTEMS, speed of movement:
Slowly: up to 15kn
Steadily: 15-25kn
Rather quickly: 25-35kn
Rapidly: 35-45kn.